The Working Lurcher

The Working Lurcher

The Traditional Skills

Jackie Drakeford

SWAN·HILL
PRESS

Dedication

This book is dedicated to Saxon, Juno and Wiz
'Swifter than Fortune . . . Sweeter than Love'

(Will H. Ogilvie)

First published in the UK in 2006
by Swan Hill Press, an imprint of Quiller Publishing Ltd

British Library Cataloguing-in-Publication Data
A catalogue record for this book
is available from the British Library

ISBN 1 904057 80 2
     978 1 904057 80 2

Typeset by Phoenix Typesetting, Auldgirth, Dumfriesshire
Printed in England by Cromwell Press, Trowbridge

Swan Hill Press

An imprint of Quiller Publishing Ltd
Wykey House, Wykey, Shrewsbury, SY4 1JA
Tel: 01939 261616 Fax: 01939 261606
E-mail: info@quillerbooks.com
Website: www.countrybooksdirect.com

'And a long, lean dog
With a sling jig-jog,
Poacher to the eyebrows, as all the lurcher clan,
Silent as a shadow, and as clever as a man'

(Patrick Chalmers)

'What a man does with his dogs is a matter for his own
conscience'

(Ted Walsh)

'Hunting and hounds were first an invention of the Gods'

(Xenophon)

Important Note

It should be clearly understood that the purpose of this book is to record lurcher work as it was carried out before the introduction of the hunting ban in February 2005. Since that time hunting with lurchers has only been legal with rabbits and rats as the quarry. All photographs in this book depicting lurchers with quarry other than rabbits or rats were taken before February 2005.

Neither the publishers nor the author can be held in any way responsible for any person breaking the law whether deliberately or in ignorance. If you are in any doubt whatsoever about what is or is not legal then you should seek legal advice.

Contents

Acknowledgements

Thanks are due to Phil Lloyd, Roly Boughton, Mike Bridle, Liz Dearden, Rob Moore, Dave Sleight, C. Welch and James Whiteman for the photographs that they have so generously supplied for inclusion in this book. Copyright remains with them in each case, and no photographs may be reproduced in any way or stored in any electronic retrieval system without prior permission in writing from the photographers concerned. Other photographs are the copyright of P. Blackman, and the author, and the same restrictions apply.

Thanks are also due to Kenneth Cassels for so generously allowing me to quote from his book *A Most Perfect Creature of Heaven*, and similarly to the British Deer Society in whose journal the piece first appeared.

This book could never have been written without the help and co-operation of the many landowners and land managers over whose land I have hunted in so many different ways, and the numerous people who have taken me hunting with their lurchers over the years. You know who you are, and I will always be grateful to you.

Most of all, thanks are due to the countless lurchers, past and present, who have shared their speed, grace and skills with me, actively co-operated with me and made endless allowances for my human clumsiness. Too many to name, your images are burned on my memory, the days and nights we shared in the fields, woods and hillsides only ever a thought away.

Prologue

urchers, sighthounds, all forms of running dog are my passion. I have written this book because legislation brought in during February 2005 threatened to make a large part of traditional lurcher work illegal in the UK. The hunting ban will come under challenge until it is repealed, but in the meantime, there is a risk of losing so much valuable information about lurcher work, because little has ever been committed to print, and much of that was fanciful. Lurcher work is conducted quietly and unobtrusively, much of it clandestinely, and even the best-known dogs have only been seen working by a very few people. Those with outstanding dogs tend to keep quiet about them as well as where and on what they are worked. Nobody wants a dog stolen or a landowner inconvenienced. Therefore I felt it necessary to record what these marvellous dogs can do, and the ways in which they do it, so that when the law changes, future generations can see what was attainable in the devastatingly efficient combination of hunter and running dog.

A hunting dog's fame seldom outlasts its lifetime, and similarly with the learning and experiences of a hunting man or woman. Everything can be lost in a single generation. This would be a tragedy, a living work of art destroyed for ever, and must not be allowed to happen. The running dog is a special part of our history.

Throughout this work, the lurcher is referred to as 'she' which is because the majority of hunters prefer to work bitches. However, male dogs have a strong following as well, and the reader is invited to understand that therefore the term covers male and female dogs equally except where stated otherwise.

At present, lurcher work continues legally in the hunting of rats and rabbits only. What the future holds is a matter of conjecture. I have written this book as if all lurcher work is still within the law, and if anybody wishes to pursue some of the skills described, I would suggest that they acquaint themselves fully with the letter of the law wherever they may be before proceeding. Otherwise, I hope you will enjoy what will be memories for some and an introduction for others, and which is intended to maintain our pride in the capabilities of our working lurchers, however bred and often 'of pedigree unknown'. This does not make them lesser beasts, but better, for only the finest are bred from, and therefore their pedigrees are written in the work of their sons and daughters.

1 Firm Foundations

Basic Standards and Experience

Working Standards

More is asked of the lurcher than possibly any other type of working dog. One discipline requires her to range far out to hunt up and find her quarry, get on terms with it and, we hope, catch it. If she does not catch, she must be willing to continue searching: if she does, she should retrieve smaller creatures to hand, or else despatch them instantly if she has caught biting quarry or something too large to retrieve. She should be biddable enough to be directed by hand signals, whistle or voice where necessary, but wise enough to work

Retrieving to hand

1

on her own initiative too. She must be talented enough to work entirely on her own, but versatile enough to become part of a pack when other dogs are involved, recognising and exploiting their abilities and dovetailing her own to fit in with them. If she goes out of sight, she should be single-minded to stick with her chosen quarry, and utterly trustworthy in the matter of livestock; furthermore she should return to her owner as soon as expedient, neither shirking nor straying. If she kills and her quarry is too big to bring back, she should return to her owner and lead him straight to it.

Other disciplines require the same dog to submerge her own will and follow the bidding of her owner. If she is lamping, the owner dictates which quarry should be run, and if it is lost, then no matter how much else there is about, the dog should return at once to her owner's side. Yet, once she is in pursuit, she needs to read her quarry's intentions while running hard, guessing where it is likely to run and boxing it away from refuge, judging when it is likely to jink and matching it when it does, and most of all, reacting to any opportunity presented for a neat pickup. By contrast, when ferreting, the dog dictates and the owner observes, for the dog is working with a scope of scent and hearing quite outside anything her owner can achieve – yet when the rabbit is caught, she should hand it over without demur, and be in position to snap up the next one – and the next after that. Many types of dog exist that are

A neat pickup (*Phil Lloyd*)

intelligent enough to work on their own initiative or biddable enough to let their human partner call the shots, but it is rare for a dog to be able to slip seamlessly between one attitude and the other, never mind doing so minute by minute in any working context.

The lurcher should not become aggressive after dealing with biting quarry, but should have the fire and commitment to kill instantly. She should have the sense and agility not to get herself injured, and the best dogs are able to tackle mink, squirrel, fox or rat without getting bitten, and deer without getting gored or kicked. Of course, there might be an odd occasion when she does get hurt, but this should be an exception rather than a regular occurrence. If catching food for the table, it should be fit to eat when it leaves her jaws, not crushed and mangled into something that is only usable for ferret food.

Physical Standards

Those are the mental attributes – now for the physical. The lurcher needs to be a sensible size for the quarry she works and the type of land that she works it on. She should have sufficient coat for the weather conditions she will be asked to perform in, but not so profuse a coat that balled-up mud and snow, or heat in summer, become a misery. A smooth coat is every bit as good as a rough one, and it is easier to see parasites and small injuries in the former, but many people like the look of a rough or broken coat. Colour is a matter of personal preference in that all colours exist in the lurcher, and 'a good dog is never a bad colour'. However, some colours show up much more than others. Brindles, blues, light merles and fawns are less easy to see over a distance, whereas both black and white can be seen from a long way away, as can the 'gay pied' (mostly white with patches of colour) and the darker varieties of merle. Time was that the black, white and pied dogs in a litter were the hardest to home because of this.

Lurcher feet need to be strong, to cope with all manner of going and gradient. 'No foot, no 'oss' is the saying from the equestrian world, and 'No foot – no dog' is equally applicable. The lurcher foot can be 'cat' or 'hare' i.e. short and round, or long, but should always be well-cushioned in the pads and strong in the knuckles. Limbs can be light or heavy according to type, but bones need to be dense and strong, and every joint should be angled in the correct manner. There is no room in the working dog world for any unsoundness, or for conformation defects that might lead to it. Loaded shoulders, weak hindlegs, poor mouths, are all serious faults.

3

Superb conformation (*J. Whiteman*)

The back should be long, level and rise to an arch over the loins, except where Bedlington or Whippet blood has given a wheel-back (which is acceptable) not a roach-back (which is not). Heart and lung space in the lurcher is contained in the depth of the brisket not the breadth of the chest: the body should be narrow and the hind-quarters wide because in galloping, the hindlegs come right forward either side of the shoulders for greatest length of stride. If a lurcher has a strong head, the quarters should be stronger in order to balance it. A long, narrow head is not a fault, as long as it fits the rest of the hound, and width of skull does not, as some say, mean that the dog is necessarily more intelligent. A long jaw is as strong as a wide jaw, for the strength lies in the masseter muscles in the cheeks. Length of jaw is more versatile in that it allows quarry of all sizes to be picked up or brought down as circumstances dictate. Teeth are extremely important, and should be of as large a size as can be accommodated correctly in the mouth, which in turn should display a scissor bite, though a level bite is acceptable.

Eyes are very important in the dog that hunts by sight. It does not

Typical merle with blue eyes

matter whether the eyes are light, dark, blue, or the flecked 'moon-pie' that comes from the collie and is common in merles, nor does it matter if the eyes are slanted from Bedlington, Deerhound or Saluki blood, but they should be large and fully functional. Eye health faults can be carried by both collies and Bedlingtons, though they are rare in a crossbreed, and if owners suspect that a dog cannot see properly, they should have a full veterinary eye check conducted. I have known several lurchers with major eye defects either genetic or from injury, and these dogs still managed to do a more than adequate job of work, though this was as much due to the intelligence of their owners in placing them correctly for their quarry as it was to the innate skills of the dogs. Skill in the handler can make all the difference to any type of working dog, creating a useful animal from the mediocre, an outstanding one from the average, and when a gifted handler and an exceptional dog form a team, then truly you will see star quality.

All in all, the lurcher should be a picture of aerodynamic

The look of eagles

symmetry and grace: 'structure governs function' as the osteopaths say. A well-made lurcher fills the eye in exactly the same way that a well-bred horse will, and for the same reason. It is difficult to look away when you see a well-made, well-conditioned hound with that 'look of eagles' about her.

But it has not always been convenient for the looks of the dog to advertise her trade – hence the shaggy-coated lurchers of old, running dogs crossed with droving dogs, their athletic lines hidden under their hair. It can take a knowledgeable eye to see what lies under the coat sometimes, or even to suspect the athletic potential of a chunky little kelpie cross, or that leggy GSD.

Shaggy-coated Bearded collie lurcher

Popular Crosses

Fashions exist in the world of the working lurcher just as they do with any other type of animal. Because a lurcher is essentially a crossbreed, albeit a very carefully planned crossbreed, different types are preferred by different people, and different crosses suit different ground and quarry. Equally, fashions come and go with one cross or another. People all have their preferences, some liking to stay with a formula that they have found works for them, while others like to experiment to see if they can find something better each time. In truth, any running dog crossed with any working dog has the potential to make a useful lurcher, and any sighthound crossed with any other sighthound will hunt like the very devil, but each breed brings its own quirks and skills, which some of us prefer and others detest, which is why the lurcher is truly a dog for all seasons. For the purists, a lurcher is a running dog/working dog cross, whereas a sighthound/sighthound cross is a longdog, but so far as I am concerned, the terms are interchangeable, as all can be trained by the right person to do a lurcher's job to a high standard, and all of 'em are 'long' dogs.

The Greyhound

The Greyhound is the cornerstone of lurcher breeding, regardless of whatever else goes into the melting pot. In the old days, obtaining the services of a Greyhound was a matter of clandestine liaison, because only certain high-ranking people were permitted to own them, such as the clergy and the gentry. Fortunately, there have always been ways around this, and many a classy Greyhound stud has been used over a poor man's working bitch. In more modern times, the advent of Greyhound racing resulted in a steady supply of cast Greyhounds of either sex that either weren't fast enough or would not race at all, all obtainable free or at a nominal price. A few

Working Greyhounds

years ago, when I wanted a young Greyhound for a friend, the reply was 'how many and what colours would he like?'. While Greyhound pups fetch a premium price, a year or so later they are given away, if they prove useless for racing. But what happens in that year? Rearing can be very good or very poor, and rearing is critical in large dogs like these. There is a lot to be said for rearing a Greyhound from a pup, if one can be obtained at a reasonable price. Sometimes there are accidental matings for which the pups are not registerable if, for instance, there are several possible sires, or sometimes if you know the right people at the right time, an unregistered pup can come your way.

Why not use a pure Greyhound instead of crossbreeding? Some people have done, with varying degrees of success. Greyhounds are certainly capable of being trained to a good standard, and can do any job a lurcher can do, but at a price. The price is their sheer speed. The Greyhound is the fastest dog in the world, and by a significant margin, has a huge prey drive, and in consequence can be very prone to injury. Foot injuries are common, and the other main cause of grief is collision, because the Greyhound is so committed to its quarry that it either does not see obstacles in its way, or does not care. Greyhounds tend to be on the big side for lurcher work, and being built for sprinting, have a reputation for being short on stamina, though some of that might be a matter of stockmanship, depending on how much stamina you actually want. For someone who works on reasonable ground and keeps away from woodland, who has the patience to retrain and socialise a cast Greyhound, and the skills on hand to treat injuries, a well-chosen Greyhound can provide a lot of fun, and will tackle any quarry. I know a woman who took on a small Greyhound bitch that would not race. Totally unsocialised, this little brindle was terrified of everything she met. She was taken ferreting, and ran away from the rabbits. She was taken coursing and ran away from the hare ('make a nice waistcoat' said one of the trainers). However, after a long programme of confidence-building, the predatory instinct at last kicked in, and she became a very useful working dog. Sadly, her speed was the death of her, and she died as the result of a full-on collision with a tree, leaving a devastated owner and many human friends, as she was a charming little thing with the gentlest of natures.

The Whippet

I really admire Whippets. They have prey drive in spades, yet they are the quietest, neatest, most gentle souls to have around when they are not working. Good ones have excellent physiques, and they are one of the few breeds where a working type can show, and a show-bred dog can work, because there is no clear physical difference between them – yet. Whippets are agile enough to chase their quarry through woodland, and fast enough to catch it, too. Their frail appearance is deceptive, for they are tough and resilient. Their small size does make some aspects of lurcher work difficult for them, for instance lack of height means that they cannot see as far as a taller dog, so anyone lamping a Whippet will have to choose their ground more carefully, but their keenness and delightful personalities make these extra considerations worthwhile. The Whippet's main virtues in lurcher breeding is to bring down the height, and add to the courage of the existing mix. Some people are dedicated to the Greyhound/Whippet cross which results in a dog smaller than the one and bigger than the other but which has lost nothing in terms of speed and drive. I once owned a lurcher which was a mixture of Greyhound, Deerhound and Whippet, and she was a delight. I have met several others since, and though it is a cross not often seen nowadays, it is still a very good mix of sighthounds.

Whippet aficionados tend to criticise the crossing of a Whippet with another small dog such as a Bedlington, or maybe a collie, and ask what such a cross can gain that makes it better than a pure Whippet. The answer is a stronger head, bigger jaw, bigger teeth, thicker skin, more coat (not always better in the case of the Bedlington, if the linty coat is inherited) and often more trainability. Some people say that Whippets tend to add noise to a lurcher mix, but I suspect that depends more on whatever is in there already and how the dog is trained and entered. I have a lot of time for Whippet crosses and have never personally found noise an issue. Purebred Whippets do have a 'scream' in them in moments of excitement, but most are silent as the grave when working. They have tremendous stamina, and great ferocity at the end of a hunt if it is needed. Many Whippets retrieve quite naturally without ever being taught, and there is a remarkable photograph in Ted Walsh's '*Longdogs by Day*' (ISBN 0 85115 266 X out of print but well worth searching for) of two Whippets carrying back a hare between them at a coursing meet.

Border Collie Cross

This is the classical cross of lurcher, which originated mainly because of the ease of finding the main ingredients, the Border collie

Border collie lurcher

and the Greyhound. Old-type collies were exclusively working dogs used for herding. They needed terrific stamina, putting in long days of work in all weathers, and often fed on little more than milk slops and porridge, unless they happened to catch a rabbit or come across some carrion. Their job was not just herding sheep but finding them as well, which means they had good noses and the ability to work hard in all weathers. Old-fashioned collies often had a soupçon of other working breeds of various sorts in them, which added to their toughness and vigour. More modern collies, though truer in the breeding, are split into a variety of sub-types, from the 'five sheep on a Sunday afternoon' triallers to the show dogs, flyball and agility types, KC Obedience dogs, or general farm workers. Some of course still work sheep on a daily basis, but these are not so easy to find. Thus the prospective lurcher owner would do well to 'gang warily' of mere words and assess if possible which type of collie has been used. There are big, heavy dogs, small, light foxy types, totally hyper ones, those that the owners claim are 'working dogs' but in fact spend most of their lives on the end of a chain, hard-eyed dogs that would face down anything, soft dogs that slink and hide, dogs that bite from fear and those that bite in the course of duty. There are also collies that never do any work of any sort. All of these can be used in the makeup of lurchers, introducing their undesirable as well as desirable traits. The value of the collie in the lurcher used to be its availability, its intelligence, tractability (not at all the same thing) toughness, endurance, longevity, coat, good feet, and the desire to work 'close' which is not to be underrated in a dog that spends much of its life working on its own initiative. Using the wrong collie, or too much collie, has the potential to breed in snappiness, hyperactivity, cowardice, neurosis, sulkiness, too much 'eye' and an unhealthy interest in sheep. Generally speaking, fifty per cent or less collie will suit most people, twenty-five per cent collie and the rest Greyhound or Greyhound/Whippet being a very handy cross that is ideal for most jobs and most owners. Anyone who cannot train one of the latter to an acceptable standard had best take up a different activity, because these are the most obliging of dogs. In many ways, this cross can be said to be the classical working lurcher as well as the base of many strains, and a good starting point for subsequent breeding. For instance, that great lurcherman Ted Walsh said that his ideal lurcher would be bred from a (Border) collie/Greyhound put to a Deerhound/Greyhound first cross. He kept a strain bred this way himself, and they were good-looking dogs that performed well in all areas. Other people have found that the Border collie cross suits them absolutely, and have never sought another type.

The first cross collie/Greyhound is remarkably consistent in looks and always smooth-coated; if then bred to another collie/Greyhound first cross, appearances are much more variable. In the same litter, some will look like collies, some very Greyhoundy, and some just like the first cross, while some pups will often be much more heavily built than others. Pups of any cross get finer in appearance and lighter in colour as they grow up, which is a useful guide to the finished article.

Bearded Collie Types

The modern Bearded collie is quite a late addition to the lurcher world, though its ancestors, the Norfolk type dogs, Smithfields, the bobtails, Original Old English and similar heavy-coated droving curs, were more likely to have been the type of dog that the squire's Greyhound covered illicitly behind the kennels in days gone by. The show-type Bearded collie is quite different from the working Bearded collie, and it is the latter which has been used most often in lurcher breeding from the last quarter of the twentieth century and beyond. Confusingly, working Beardies that actually herd are now very rare, but the strain has been kept going by dedicated aficionados, and is still referred to as 'working'. They are lighter-

Norfolk type

Smithfield type

built and with less coat than show Beardies, more intelligent and, because of that, more demanding. They have been bred to find and face down very independent stock, often in hard conditions of weather and terrain, and can be pretty independent themselves. The ample rough coat and plethora of colours make this a very attractive animal visually, which is the source of much of its popularity in modern lurcher breeding, along with its toughness and dura-bility. The Beardie coat does have its downside, however, needing more than average grooming if the dog is to be kept comfortable, and is apt to ball up in mud or snow. Half Beardie half Border is also a well-known cross to put with a Greyhound, and many modern lurchers are bred this way, notably from the Hancock kennels in Sutton Coldfield.

Kelpies and Cattle Dogs

These are two more herding breeds which are used in the creation of a specific style of lurcher, though neither is common. The cattle dog crosses, one of the best known being pest controller Phil Lloyd's

Phil Lloyd's 'Speckle' cattle dog lurcher *(Phil Lloyd)*

Cattle dog lurcher – a real predator *(Phil Lloyd)*

inimitable Speckle, were created because of the punishing nature of the ground that he worked in Hampshire, where flints and gravel ask a lot of a dog's feet, and working dense woodland needs a dog with as much common sense as prey drive, which is not so easy with a running dog type. Some of us can pick the ground we work our dogs on, but a professional cannot, and so the first cross cattle dog/Greyhound came about. Phil will be the first to say that these are not the dog for everyone because they are so precocious and strong-minded, with a prey-drive so primitive and overwhelming that they demand constant vigilance and careful training. After working two generations of cattle dog crosses with great success, Phil chose to return to his first love, the collie cross. His cattle dog crosses are shown working impressively on the Moucher Productions videos. (Moucher Productions, PO Box 372, Southampton SO14 OTA, England.) A few other people still work cattle dog crosses, or have crossed cattle dog into the lurcher mix, but it remains something of a rarity and is not the type of dog for a beginner, being splendid in the right hands as Phil has proved, but a nightmare in the wrong ones.

The kelpie crosses, best known being those bred by Dave Sleight and appearing in his Lurcher Roadshow at the summer country shows and game fairs, are also formidable workers, and generally

Kelpie/Whippet lurcher

Kelpie/Greyhound lurcher

considered to be the equal of the Border collie cross in terms of intelligence and tractability. Deceptive in appearance, the first crosses are quite thickset, especially those that go back to Whippet lineage rather than Greyhound. They certainly can perform though, and kelpie crosses have several times won the prestigious Lurcher Field Trials held every winter, for which the qualification process involves passing a stiff obedience test before even getting out into the field. Dave's kelpie crosses can be seen working in his two videos (Lurcher Fieldcraft and Purdey's Progress).

Kelpie and cattle dogs are very different from each other, which is one reason why several other lurcher breeders are now producing kelpie crosses, but very few try a second cattle dog cross after the first. Both are strong, intelligent dogs, built for endurance rather than speed, and for best results, needing an owner at least as smart as they are. Where a collie/Greyhound will succeed, so will these: they are a dog for a particular range of work, and offer very specific skills. They are tough, with endless stamina and have very good feet; they need plenty of work and occupation, and are fiercely loyal. Not a dog for the weekend hunter, they need owners who can offer them as much commitment as the dogs themselves, and on difficult ground, in difficult conditions, rabbiting day in day out, this type of lurcher has earned a very devoted following.

Saluki Types

The Saluki brings phenominal stamina and toughness into any lurcher cross. Instantly recognisable, Saluki blood gives a delicate-looking light, narrow build and often long, low-set ears, long-toed feet that can act on any going, and large slanting eyes, with a silken coat that can be short like a Greyhound's, or else typically fringed on ears, tail and feet. The mental attributes of the Saluki are intriguing: such dogs are stubborn and sensitive in equal part, which can make them very challenging to train and unforgiving of human weaknesses. Saluki crosses will not tolerate any kind of rough or unjust treatment, and will simply withdraw into themselves and refuse to co-operate with a handler they dislike. They do not take easily to a change of owner, but frequently get moved on because of this intransigent character. With an owner as intelligent as they are – which is very – and who is perceptive and sensitive, they become strongly bonded, and have the ability to get inside your mind to a degree that few other dogs can match. Win a Saluki cross's trust and she will do anything for you: break it and she will only please herself. Possessed of a strong prey drive as well as prey sense,

17

Purebred Saluki working

that intuitive grasp of what quarry is about to do with the corres-
ponding inborn ability to match it, the Saluki cross can be the
ultimate hunter or a something liability at the spin of Fate's coin.
Beginners can make good dogs out of them, just as experienced
lurcher owners of a certain mindset can fail utterly, for they demand
sensitive and consistent handling. Lacking the hair-trigger response
of the collie cross, they can infuriate some owners by the hesitation
before they respond to a command, but this is just their way. As the
collie crosses naturally work close, so the Saluki type naturally
ranges far, therefore a quantity of Saluki blood means that the dog
will cover a lot of ground in search of quarry, but may well be out
of sight when she finds it, unless the owner has instilled some basic
training. It is from this that the Saluki's reputation for running off
and being unreliable in recall comes. They can be trained to come
back perfectly well, but it takes a lot more work than with the collie
crosses. They are not the dog for anyone who is not in control of
themselves, who gives in to peer pressure, or who thinks training is
achieved with shouting and threats, and equally they are not the
dog for weak or inadequate personalities. They respond with
delight to kindness and quiet firmness, will work with you rather
than for you, and will share the darkest secrets of the primitive

world if you only want to learn. There is little that a Saluki cross cannot tackle with success, despite their apparently fragile appearance. Fifty per cent or more of Saluki in a lurcher demands a very special type of owner, but a lesser dash of Saluki in any cross will leaven the most pedestrian mixture into something a little out of the ordinary. If you work a Saluki cross, your hunting days and nights will stay burned in your memory for ever, probably in equal measure of delighted awe and acute embarrassment.

The Saluki cross, or predominantly Saluki/Greyhound, is the dog of choice for hare coursing in big country such as the Fens. There, these dogs can course as their desert-bred ancestors did (and still do) taking their time because they have the space to do so. They do not have to bring the course to a rapid end because the quarry is heading for woodland or other cover. There is still cover on the Fens, and hares will readily take to drains, rabbit holes or game cover crops if under pressure, but many choose to challenge the dog on their own ground, confident of their superior speed, stamina and agility to beat the predator. And most of them succeed. It takes a very good, very fit dog to catch consistently on the Fens, and the names of those that do are passed down like legends through the generations of their descendents.

This does not mean that all the Saluki cross can do is course. Breeders such as 'Stat' Stainton and Penny Taylor consistently produce lurchers that not only perform outstandingly well as Fen coursers, they can do other jobs as well. There are dashes of other blood, such as Deerhound and collie, in the makeup of these dogs, and they are capable of performing well and consistently in a variety of disciplines all over the UK. Many people who course, however, keep their dogs for that job alone, and so Saluki/Greyhound is bred to Saluki/Greyhound, with nothing else added, resulting in dogs that look like rough or smooth Salukis or else Greyhounds with suspiciously long ears, domed skulls and just a touch of feather to the tail.

Deerhound Types

Back in the nineteen-seventies, this was one of the most popular lurcher types, especially the second cross i.e. the Deerhound / Greyhound to a Deerhound / Greyhound. These dogs typically have long all-terrain feet, short hard weatherproof broken coats, a pronounced occipital bump at the back of the skull, and a giveaway short ruff down each side of the neck which differs from the wider collie-cross ruff that usually goes all round. Some devotees have

Deerhound lurcher

Second cross Deerhound lurcher

Purebred Deerhound
(*C. Welch*)

never looked any further than this majestic lurcher, which can do any job but is particularly well suited to fox and deer work. Though slow to mature, and often not fully grown until three years old, these dogs are easy to train and have around with none of the hyper attitude of the collie types, or the unforgiving nature of the Saluki cross. They do have that momentary sighthound pause when given a command, as if considering whether it is worth their while to obey, but they are kind, biddable dogs and usually glad to oblige. They also have quite a sense of humour, and it is a rare Deerhound lurcher that has not tripped her owner up quite deliberately, in the same way that she would trip a deer if the opportunity arose. Similarly, I have seen Deerhound crosses bring down much heavier dogs while playing, and doing it so fast that the human eye could not follow precisely what took place. In my mind's eye there is a mainly white Deerhound-bred lurcher which specialised in spinning her two Rottweiller friends over, and only a few weeks ago, one of her descendents did exactly the same when attacked by a large stray dog while we were out ferreting. Though this other dog was several stone heavier, she flicked it over effortlessly onto its back where it thrashed about like a giant beetle, and when it got up it had had all the fight knocked out of it by that one manoeuvre.

People who have not had much to do with Deerhound-bred dogs

21

assume that they are clumsy because of their size, and cannot turn well, but this is not so. I have seen purebred Deerhounds at work, and been amazed at their agility, length of stride and turning capabilities, not to mention their extraordinary leaping power. I know one of these which can leap from a standstill to his own height over a six-foot man, reach out and tap him on the head with a giant paw and twist to land lightly facing the other way. The Deerhound lurcher retains this agility, and is even quicker on the turn with the size brought down. They eat ground when they stretch out to run, and many is the quarry that does not even get the chance to turn, so quickly is the hound upon it.

So long as they are not worked too hard too young, but allowed to grow on slowly, the Deerhound cross will fill the biggest boots, and the largest freezer as well. First crosses are relatively short-lived, generally lasting until twelve or so, but the second crosses commonly go well into their teens. Last year I lost my remaining Deerhound second cross, just short of her eighteenth birthday; though weary from years, she had caught her last rabbit only a few months before. Admittedly this was pegged in long grass, but shows she still had a good nose and had lost none of her strike.

Probably the only reason the Deerhound cross has lost popularity is the rarity of the raw materials, for purebred Deerhounds are being bred very large nowadays, much larger than their true job warrants. Perhaps, too, impatience has something to do with it, for not everyone will wait so long for a dog to mature when other crosses are in full work so much sooner. Nevertheless, the Deerhound, in whatever percentage, offers a lot to the lurcher, and I like to have Deerhound blood in my dogs, not just for their beauty, symmetry, coat and good feet, but because there is something in their nature and mine that goes well together.

Terrier Cross

The classic terrier lurcher used in lurcher breeding is the Bedlington, for its natural silence while working, ferocious prey drive (truly a wolf in sheep's clothing), large skull and teeth, and running-dog shape. Bedlingtons are often crossed with Whippets, giving even more fire and speed, and the attitude of coming back with their shield or on it. These little hunters are absolutely fearless, sometimes to their detriment. They have excellent noses, are very companionable, and easy to train. The downside is the coat, for the linty Bedlington coat is not weatherproof, and picks up all manner of detritus when working cover – and oh boy! do they work cover.

Bedlington type – large skull and teeth

If you have a Bedlington cross, you will spend a lot of time picking thorns out of her.

Crossed with Greyhound or a larger lurcher to give more size, the Bedlington will work any quarry, but their speciality is fox, which they will despatch with almost holy fervour. They are tough, versatile dogs, with the quick, terrier temperament, which the owner will sometimes have to watch with other dogs, as Beddy crosses don't suffer fools gladly, or even at all. They don't start fights but can be very reactive if attacked, or even approached with the wrong body language. The Bedlington lurcher wears her heart on her sleeve: what you see is what you get, and what you get is a cracking little dog. I have had one for the last nine years, and enjoyed every minute.

Other terrier crosses do exist, and at time of writing, there is quite a revival for the Wheaten terrier, which breeds a very attractive-looking lurcher, somewhat heavier and more powerful than the Bedlington type. Any terrier breed will put in fire and prey drive, but some are not as intelligent as others, and some tend to be noisy, while others can be very stubborn. The speed of a Greyhound and the intransigence of some terrier breeds can make for quite a handful of dog.

Bull Crosses

Although the bull breeds are referred to as 'Bull terriers' I am covering them separately from other terriers as their name is really a contraction of 'bull and terrier' the old fighting breeds where the quickness of the terrier was allied to the power of the old-style Bulldog. At time of writing, this is a cross that seems to be very popular, the 'bull' side being Staffordshire, preferably the leggier 'Irish Staffordshire' (not KC recognised) rather than English. The Pit Bull is no longer legally available for breeding in UK, though there can be no doubt that Pit blood runs in the veins of many bull cross lurchers.

The first cross results in a strong dog with great breadth of chest, skull and jaw, which in the best is balanced with equally strong quarters. If the quarters taper away as they do in many specimens, the dog cannot work as a lurcher because it cannot gallop, as the hindquarters need to propel the hindlegs forward of the front legs in the galloping stride. The physical ability to do this is thwarted by

Bull cross – heavily built and straight in the shoulder

the big skull, barrel ribcage, broad chest and wide back. For this reason, many bull crosses are apt to sustain early damage to shoulders and feet, because they have to pull themselves forward with their forelegs rather than driving from the rear. This, with the broad heavy head, also tends to load the shoulders, a fault exacerbated by some owners, who tend to think that the dogs look better when over-muscled in front. Once the shoulders have started to load, the elbows turn out to compensate, and the wrists start to weaken, hastening the ruination of the feet, which tend to splay early on in their career. They are not the fastest of dogs, nor the best for turning ability, as even their stoutest fans will admit. Crossed back again to Greyhound, you get, not surprisingly, a better dog, fairly athletic and with tremendous strength and endurance.

It should be remembered that in the late 1700s, Lord Orford crossed Bulldog into his Greyhounds to give them more drive, and every Greyhound alive today traces back to his famous coursing bitch Czarina, who never lost a course. However, the Bulldogs that Lord Orford used were a long-lost type, athletic and game enough to drive and hold bulls in the markets and slaughterhouses, and he needed to cross back to Greyhound many times after the outcross to lose the more undesirable characteristics. More recently, a century or so ago, Whippets had the occasional outcross to Staffordshire Bull terrier, the results of which still crop up in Whippets with unusually broad skulls and chests, and prominent eyes. Of all sighthounds, Whippets can be the noisiest, some strains emitting very Bull terrier type shrieks when excited, and maybe their outstanding courage also owes a lot to the influence of those early outcrossings.

Modern bull crosses can be trained to a good standard, and are people-friendly, straightforward dogs, though many show a marked antipathy to other dogs, and will take the fight to them. Physically, they retain the broad chest and skull through two or three generations of Greyhound blood, and the half-crosses when kept at running weight can look grotesquely thin in comparison to more traditional lurcher types. There is a school of thought that asks if the bull cross is really a lurcher at all, whether it is right to ask such a dog to run for its living when physically it is so ill-designed for it, and which of a true lurcher's tasks it can perform better or even as well as any of the other established crosses. Given that the main attribute that separates any kind of lurcher from a mongrel is its speed, the answer is food for thought. The bull crosses have many dedicated fans, and the best are magnificent-looking dogs, but whether they are lurchers or not is a matter I will leave you to ponder.

GSD cross

Other Crosses

All sorts of other working dogs have been tried in lurcher breeding, the most popular of the minority types being gundogs and German Shepherd Dogs (GSDs). They all have their followings, and can be useful lurchers with the added advantage that they do not attract so much attention as the racier-shaped animals. Generally, a second cross of running dog is required to lift the mixture away from the heaviness of the base breeds and make a more versatile lurcher, because all the will in the world is worth little if not harnessed to a physique that is capable of doing the job. Gundogs and GSDs are at least as plentiful as collies, but remain a minority cross in lurcher breeding, which answers the unspoken question about whether they make a better lurcher.

Changes

In the latter part of the twentieth century, the lurcher's role changed from that of the poaching and mouching cur to as near respectable as it has ever been. Once used – and still used – to put meat on the table, the lurcher also became invaluable in her role of vermin catcher, not only for animals such as the rabbit and fox, but for more recently imported pest species such as mink and grey squirrel. Lurchers were not only used by professionals, such as gamekeepers and pest controllers, but by people every bit as dedicated who hunted in their spare time (and, speaking as one who has fallen asleep in the odd business meeting, time that wasn't so spare either). These hobby hunters provided a free vermin control service to farmers and other landowners, and frequently also gave welcome help to the professionals too. The lurcher became appreciated as never before, for her multiple talents, intelligence and biddability, as well as her courage and beauty. For those who kept their lurchers as part of the family or as a constant companion rather than kennelled when not being exercised or at work, there was an added appreciation of the lurcher's extraordinarily sweet nature, largely the gift of the Greyhound ancestor, sometimes in smaller part from other running dogs as well. Lurchers get inside your mind, and if allowed are almost spiritual in their link with their owner.

Many people kept their own family of lurchers, carefully bred to suit the particular terrain and quarry of the area, and several kennels bred commercially for the lurcher market. Most of these, private or

'Bitsa' lurcher, and none the worse for it

commercial, were readily identifiable by type, and lurcher aficionados would know exactly what was meant by, for instance, a Hancock, a Burrell, a Docherty, a Sleight or a Platts dog. As with other branches of dogdom, there were fashions in lurcher breeding, everybody being keen to promote their particular favourite, whether Border collie, Bearded x Border collie, Deerhound, Bedlington terrier, Saluki or Bull terrier bred, with a staunch corner being held for the 'Bitsa' which had so many breeds in its makeup that it was best described as 'bitsa this and bitsa that'. Each cross has its own strengths and weaknesses, and with so much to choose from, everyone could get a lurcher to suit, if only they were astute enough to know what they needed, and indeed what they did not.

Breed Options

Finding the purebreds to make up the lurcher mix was not always so easy, and as the show-type dogs ranged further away from their working antecedents, so more people concentrated on breeding lurcher to lurcher, proven worker to proven worker, to get the results that they needed. Where working strains existed in the pure

Heather brindle Deerhound lurcher second cross

breeds, they were eagerly sought after, such as the Ardkinglas line of Scottish Deerhounds which had an outcross to Greyhound in the early part of the twentieth century, courtesy of Anastasia Noble, who kept and bred the Ardkinglas hounds. These were tested most thoroughly in the field as well as being shown, as were certain other lines in the Deerhound group, making the breed as a whole all the better for the rigours of real work. It is sad that some of the ancient colours seem to have been lost in the Deerhound: one does not find now the oatmeal, fawn, bright brindle and even pied coats, nor the white with red ears beloved of old legend, though this last does turn up in the occasional lurcher litter, and I bred one myself in 1991 from putting two Deerhound cross lurchers together. That litter also threw that most lovely of Deerhound colours, the heather brindle, in a dog that looked like a pure Deerhound of the old style, a mere 29 inches high compared to the show-ring giants, and all in proportion. This particular dog was a great worker to all quarry, but particularly deer, and it was a great sadness to me that his owner never bred from him.

Salukis had their coursing strains, and the type was well-kept, as was the case with Whippets, many of which coursed, raced and showed. Greyhounds, both coursing and racing, were freely available for breeding, but they were not always the most fertile of dogs, nor all that easy to breed, as most bitches would only come on heat once a year, and some less often than that, with a few that would not come in at all. Coursing Greyhounds were better tested than racers, as the former would use their mouths, intelligence and instincts on real quarry in the field, whereas the racing Greyhound, though smaller and lighter and thus preferable in terms of physique, would be an unknown quantity in these terms. So far as speed was concerned, there was little difference between a Greyhound that won a race, and the rest that did not: they are still the fastest dogs in the world, but coursing Greyhounds are every bit as fast – some would say faster – and had to show more stamina as well as twist and turn after their hares, and to strike when the chance came to end the course. Greyhounds that won courses were not necessarily the best ones for lurcher breeding, as pure speed is less important in lurcher circles than agility and strike, but astute lurcher breeders would keep an eye on dogs that showed these abilities and would often be able to acquire them for a small sum of money, or even free, because they did not win their courses.

The loss of coursing Greyhounds to the gene pool of the lurcher should not be underrated, but the racing Greyhounds will also give speed, symmetry and prey drive, even if they have not had the opportunity of being tested in the field. Show Greyhounds are

29

another kettle of fish entirely, being too big and heavy and with incorrect conformation for a working dog. Looking uneasily into the future for a moment, the lurcher as a type is only safe while there are field-tested Greyhounds, Salukis, Deerhounds and Whippets to use as a starting point, as well as working roles for the base breeds such as collies and terriers. There are already, as mentioned earlier, several sub-types of Border collie, from the general farm dog to the trialling kind, obedience dogs, agility dogs, show dogs and working hill collies. Each has a slightly different physique, but more importantly, a different mindset, and some of those attitudes are not the sort that you want in a lurcher. A good Greyhound can and will lift whatever base qualities are lacking into the state of grace that is a working lurcher, but even the sound, kind nature of the Greyhound is not necessarily enough to overcome the character deficiencies in certain strains of cold-blood dog, and unless such dogs are tested in the field rather than in highly-stylised amusements, their inadequacies can remain hidden for long enough to pass into the gene pool of the lurcher. Lurcher to lurcher matings may bring these less desirable qualities to the surface in one or more of the pups, if they are lying latent in both parents, or else a random unlucky working incident or a less than good owner might be enough to bring to the surface some trait that would otherwise have lain safely dormant.

Choosing the Right Dog

You do not get perfection in any living beast, no, not even in yourself. Do not think that the lurchers of old were perfect either, nor the people who trained them. But they were very effective at their various jobs. The modern lurcher can be every bit as good, possibly better, because we know that much more about general care and training, and are prepared to persevere through a training hiccup rather than as in harsher times, write the dog off and start again. So, what do you need, what is essential, and what can you work around?

First of all, look at the ground and quarry that you intend to work. There is much made of a dog being an 'all-rounder' but this means different things to different people. So long as the dog is capable and willing to do the tasks that the owner wants of it, that is quite all-round enough. In truth, each dog will have certain strengths and weaknesses, which the astute trainer will be able to develop in the first case and strengthen in the second.

Choosing the right breeding for your dog goes a long way to

getting the animal that you want. If you are lucky, you will know both parents and have seen them working, maybe even the offspring of a previous litter, but that is the ideal, and many people know no more than whatever the owners tell them – which in some cases demands the proverbial pinch of salt. If you have a good eye for conformation, and can pick out the various breeds in your proposed lurcher's parents, then you are likely to get a decent dog. Do not go by the appearance of a very young pup, as they change constantly while growing: instead, pick a bright healthy pup that has clearly had a good start in life, for it takes a long time to make up ground lost if a pup has not been well kept. If the mother looks in good condition, the premises are clean and the pups are lively and keen to meet you, that is a good beginning. The pups should not have any trace of discharge from eyes, nose, mouth or rear end, nor should they be pot-bellied and stare-coated with worms. While all pups will have worms to some degree, conscientious breeders will have started a worming programme for the new owners to continue, and will be able to tell you what they have used and when. Do be sure to use a proper wormer from your vet, not the sort that can be bought over the counter in a pet shop, because the latter simply aren't man enough for the job. Worm infestation can cause extensive gut damage if left untreated, which will mean that your dog may suffer from digestive problems and also not be able to get maximum benefit from her food. Well-reared pups from well-kept bitches start life with a big bonus in health. A working dog needs a strong constitution: no matter how well-bred; if she has not got the physical strength to do her job, your life together will be a long run of strains, sprains and maybe even fractures. Injuries are a part of any working dog's life, but the strong dog will recover faster and better than the weaker one, and innate health of joints and tendons may make the difference between a day off work, or a month and a vet visit.

Socialising

It is perfectly possible to make a useful dog out of an under-socialised pup, but it is a lot harder. Lurcher pups are big, often noisy, and lively, and after the first three weeks, the only way to survive is to transfer them to a kennel and run, so don't be put off by the pups not being reared in the home. Good breeders will still take the pups into the home to accustom them to domestic noise and bustle, and also see to it that the pups meet as many people and other animals as possible. Such pups are streets ahead of those reared in a shed with no introduction to life-proofing. Even if you live in the back of beyond and don't plan to meet many people, there may be times when your dog is exposed to civilisation, especially if you cannot care for her due to ill health, or a sudden problem that takes you away for some reason. If your pup has started her social-isation programme with her breeder, then she is far more likely to bond with you, which in turn makes her much easier to train than a pup which does not care one way or another for humans, having only seen one for a short time each day while food and water is put in and muck taken out. I know a good dog man who spent months working on a pup like this. She would not come to him for the first eight weeks, and even at two years old showed little in the way of affection. She became very fond of her owner, but was unable to show it, and a lesser person would never have been able to train her to the standard that he managed to achieve in the end. Make life easy: pick a well-bred well-reared pup and it will take half the work to achieve success.

Speed, Size and Stamina

How much speed does your dog need for the quarry she works and the ground she has to work over? Fast dogs injure themselves more

Bred for tremendous stamina and all-terrain capability *(Phil Lloyd)*

than slow dogs from the sheer speed at which they connect with obstacles, and are best worked on open ground and good going. Slower dogs will handle rough ground and steep gradients with less mishap, though can be left looking flat-footed on fast ground. It is tempting to think that large dogs need more turning space than small dogs, and though this is true to some extent, if a big dog is what you need, you will find them surprisingly agile for their size. Even purebred Deerhounds can spin around in far less space than you would imagine, and are generally very quick on their feet. Athletic in the leap, and with an awesomely long stride, these hounds and their first crosses are designed for larger quarry but can acquit themselves surprisingly well on smaller beasts. However, if most of your work is on rabbits, you would be better with less height in your dog. Small dogs by contrast, while able to fit into small spaces and turn with astonishing dexterity, cannot see very far on rough ground because of their height (get down to the dog's level and you'll see exactly what I mean) so while they can excel at, for instance, ferreting, open-land running and woodland hunting, if the bulk of your work is lamping or rough-ground coursing, a taller dog will find the job easier.

Stamina is a very personal requirement. Just how much stamina do you need? Relatively few people nowadays are going to work their dog for more than a few hours at a time, and there is no point in having a dog with stamina to burn if it is at the expense of other attributes. Most people need to fit their dog work in with other commitments, so a dog with endless stamina that cannot be left for part of each day while the owner gets on with human tasks is likely to be a liability rather than a pleasure. Even professional 'pesters' need to take the odd day off. Think well before you acquire a dog that can keep going all day or night, day after day, because you will need to be able to do that as well. Healthy lurchers will have enough stamina for a day's ferreting, a few hours of lamping or bushing, or to run a number of good courses, provided they are fit enough in the first place, and sensibly rested. Recovery rate is different from stamina, and very much related to fitness: as a generalisation, dogs with a good recovery rate can be fast or slow, but stamina dogs are seldom particularly fast except in the case of the Saluki crosses. The great advantage of the sprinter over the stayer is in the hours that you do not work her, for then she will rest comfortably until you take her out again, instead of pacing and whining and generally looking for occupation.

Strength

A lurcher does not need bulk or brawn. She is essentially a dog that catches with speed, cunning, nose, strike or all of them. A proper lurcher can bring quarry to book using a lurcher's skills, and anyone who claims that bodily strength is essential is either using the wrong dog or working the wrong quarry.

In the Mind

Having chosen a pup that is bred the right way for the job you want to do, think about the mental attributes that you need, not just for the work but so that you and the dog gel together. Lurchers are gentle and sensitive, but some crosses can also be monumentally stubborn. Some are very much more intelligent than others; an intelligent dog does not necessarily catch more game, but it will catch it differently, and again this may not suit some owners. If you find overt intelligence irritating in people, you will find it even more so in a dog, and the same goes for the more pedestrian dog with the intellectual owner. Prey drive and prey sense are a long way from problem-solving intelligence, and not always found in equal measure. It is a rare dog that has all three of these attributes, and a rarer owner that can bring the best out of such an animal. So look in the mirror, be honest about what you want and whether you can

Prey drive and prey sense

deal with it, and don't be tempted to kit yourself out with a high-performance, high-octane model when a nippy runabout will suit you better.

Lucky Dip

A lot of us take on dogs not knowing much about their background, perhaps from one of the dog rescue places, or the friend of a friend who has to change his lifestyle to one that does not accommodate a dog. Some people move on their older dogs to make room for younger ones, and while I cannot agree with this, it is possible to get a well-trained, experienced worker that way, albeit one that will only have a couple more full working years left in her. Maybe you have lost a dog in a tragic accident, and the new season is coming up fast: you are committed to your pest control duties and will lose your permission if you do not work it. Perhaps you were not intending to take on another dog at all, but circumstances brought you together and you could not turn her away. These dogs can be so rewarding: one of the best dogs I ever had came from the dog rescue. However, most of them come with 'baggage', emotional, physical or both, and it can take a while to untangle the behaviours that you want from the ones that you do not. It amazes me that people think they can just pick up the end of the lead and the dog will trust them, obey them and work for them straight away. All this is something that you have to earn, and the journey can be very frustrating at times. To describe how to achieve a good working relationship with a second-hand dog would take up too much of this book; suffice it to say that you will need great patience and so will the dog, and both of you will have to make allowances for each other. In all but a very few cases, you will end up with a devoted and loyal companion and fellow hunter, for the price of time taken with settling in. The dog may have enduring physical problems from being worked too young or from untreated injury, and she might always be afraid of certain types of human dress, voice or behaviour, but that is little enough, after all.

Standards

Having found the right pup, you need to spend the first year on basic training and socialisation. This is not a lazy option, for the work that you do in the first year will reap you dividends for ever after, whereas if you don't bother, you will have a dog that cannot realise anything like her true potential. If you do the job properly, that first year will be a busy one, believe me. By the end of it, you should have a dog that is unfazed by crowds, children, noise and other animals, is completely steady to all forms of livestock and cats, and will obey voice commands, whistles and hand signals. Even if you are a good whistler with your mouth, it is worth buying a whistle, because the sound carries well to the dog and is less noticeable to humans, should you be wishing to be discreet. Each whistle sounds different, though the human ear is not so good at hearing these differences. Dogs have to be trained to respond to a whistle: I remember a gundog trainer friend who was out walking with his three Labradors one day when he saw a woman and her dogs approaching him, her dogs pulling hard. He blew his whistle and his dogs sat, then he blew a recall and they all came back and sat beside him. As you may imagine, the woman was impressed. 'I must get a whistle like that' she said.

The dog should be sufficiently responsive to be called off forbidden quarry, or else not go on it in the first place. Don't expect miracles here, because sometimes an animal will jump up under the dog's nose and she will be in full flight before she herself has registered what it is. However, this being the case (and take it from me, this WILL be the case) the dog should either stop on your command, or stop herself as soon as she realises. I have seen a very

Steady with sheep

36

Steady with horses (*Roly Boughton*)

embarrassed lurcher pull up after launching herself onto an Irish setter that looked very like a roebuck, and once had three pull up simultaneously after an intellectually challenged rabbit-coloured cat chose to run across an open field in front of them.

It is useful, indeed, may one day save her life, if your dog will drop into a 'down' on command, will stay until released from that by another command, will wait, ready for the next instruction, can be stopped in a particular place, will retrieve and hold until you can take whatever has been brought back, and will lie down and stay, both close to you and at a distance. If your lurcher, running in with a retrieve, can be stopped and made to lie down still holding that retrieve, and then bring it in to you when you want, it can save a lot of embarrassment, believe me. Similarly, if a dog can be sent forward or brought back behind when you want, will walk and trot to heel without tripping you up, and will cast off and hunt to either side of you as well as go back, this is immensely useful.

You should be able to leave the dog in position while you go out of sight, for instance one side of a hedge or fence, knowing that the dog will be where you left her when you get back. Personally, I don't mind if they move around a little, but the exercise should start by aiming for immobility. When the overall training standard is as you want it, you can then cut the dog a little slack here and there, which is particularly important in the 'stay' because while you might need the dog as long-stop while you (for instance) beat some cover towards her, you want her to have enough initiative to break her 'stay' if someone tries to get hold of her, and also to go on the quarry that you flush as soon as it appears. This is the real challenge of training the working lurcher, because one minute you need instant obedience, and the next requires the dog to make her own decisions.

You should work within the lurcher's physique and natural responses. That long back does not make the 'sit' position easy, and while some lurchers will offer you a natural 'sit' others find it very uncomfortable. That being the case, forget teaching the 'sit' and concentrate on your dog being immobile either standing or lying down. Similarly, a deep brisket means that lying down in the conventional 'couchant' position soon becomes uncomfortable, so you should not consider it disobedience if the dog chooses to sprawl on her side after a while. Most lurchers are naturally furtive beasts, and will warn you if another person is approaching by slinking to your side. Some will rumble a soft growl, and I have one who will stand between me and the approaching visitor and bark a serious warning (this can be awkward if it is your friendly landowner or 'keeper who has given you permission to be there, but in my experience, lurchers are very astute at telling friend from foe).

Jumping

Depending on where and what you work, it may be more or less important that the lurcher jumps. Early lurcher books were insistent on all dogs jumping, which spawned a lot of lurchers injured in wrists and shoulders from being jumped too young, too high or too much. Some people even started their lurchers jumping when they were tiny puppies, and there was the impression that your lurcher was a crock of ordure if she wasn't clearing five-bar gates while still in nappies. It is not so much what goes up as what comes down that causes issues with jumping. The dog lands on one front leg, usually the same front leg. If the landing is hard or uneven, it is possible for a dog to injure that leg, and if the dog is less than full-grown, it is very likely that damage will be done to her joints. Lurchers are great athletes and some of them jump for fun, but that is very different from making them jump. 'Over, under, round or through' should

A time to jump . . . (*Roly Boughton*)

. . . and a time to go through

be the lurcher motto, and the dog which jumps only when there is no other way across an obstacle is going to last a lot longer than the one that is told to jump every time.

There are other reasons for not teaching jumping early. Adolescent lurchers go through a bolshie stage, and it is a lot easier to cope with the ones that run off if they do not realise that they can leap. One of mine set off after three Fallow deer once, even though I had told her not to, but as they could jump the stock-fence and she could not, that little bit of defiance did not cause any harm. Jumping is also a big cause of accidents, particularly at night, and a lurcher that jumps into an unsafe landing is a liability when lamping. I know of a great many lurchers that died as a result of jumping onto farm machinery, into a hidden dip, onto dumped rubbish of the glass, wire and rusting metal kind, and even once onto a passing car, but I do not know of a single lurcher that died as a result of not jumping. Teach the dog to jump when it is close to a year old and you will have a stronger dog for all of her life. And in case you wonder whether I practise what I preach, my current young dog was a little besom for jumping the baby-gate that supposedly kept her in, not to mention being a regular on the table and the window-sill. Still, I did not ask her to jump more than small obstacles when out, and not long ago, found a field full of rabbits where the fence was a mere three feet high in one place. That was the place I sent her over, and waited for her return. I watched her come back to me with a glow of pride as she retrieved her rabbit, then thought, 'She isn't going for the low place,' for she floated over the fence at its full five feet of height while I was still thinking 'she isn't slowing down'. So there you have it – be careful with your dog's jumping!

Handling

You will bless the days you spent grooming and handling your dog all over, for there may come a time when you have an injured dog and need to hand her over to strangers to care for. They will then bless you as well. Even routine veterinary work is far easier on everybody if the dog is used to being examined. Right from the start, familiarise your dog with having eyes, ears, mouth and genitals inspected, with being brushed, having nails cut, being rolled over to examine the underneath, and every toe opened out so that you can peer between them. Handle firmly, don't tickle and don't hurt, and reward your dog with a titbit and your approval after she has submitted to being peered at. Keep sessions short, never hurt the

A hand on the collar

dog when checking her, and she will soon learn to allow these inspections with good grace. Also, get your dog used to the concept of gentle restraint before she is ill, because there may be times when she is shocked and distressed, and you have to hold her for someone else to help her, maybe free her from being painfully caught up, or give emergency veterinary treatment. Get her used to your hand on her collar or scruff in a non-confrontational manner, just part of a caress: some dogs only ever feel a hand on the neck as a prelude for being scolded or hurt, but one day you may need to catch hold of her to save her life, and you don't want her shying away from your hands. If ever a dog is in a situation where it is caught up and panicking, for instance caught in a fence that it has jumped badly, remember that even the nicest dog can fear-bite in pain and distress. Get something in the dog's mouth that isn't you: a big stick that won't splinter, or a rolled-up item of clothing. While she is biting on that, you can lift her and free her without risk to yourself.

Recall

A working lurcher must, above all, return to you at once as soon as you command, and should come right up to hand. If you do not teach anything else, teach her that, and never, ever punish her after she has come up to you. Don't use her name when scolding her (you will find plenty of other useful words) for her name should always be a sound that gives her pleasure and security, and you do not want her learning to fear the sound of it.

Faults

'To their virtues ever kind, to their faults a little blind' is the saying, as true for dogs as for the horses for which it was originally written. There are a few behaviours which are considered faults in the working lurcher, and which are incurable. How much they bother the individual hunter varies, and any fault should not be seen in isolation, but as a part of the whole dog i.e. do the good attributes make it worth tolerating one major fault? The answer is different for each one of us.

Opening Up

This is the term given to a dog that barks or yelps when running after quarry. Sometimes such dogs are referred to as 'yappers' or 'yippers'. While in some breeds, such as the Foxhound, 'running mute' is a fault, a noisy lurcher is anathema to most lurchermen and women. The whole ethos of lurcherdom is its silence. Opening up can be inborn, especially if one or both parents yip, or it can be brought out by clumsy entering (the dog that barks at a fox instead of tackling it because she is afraid), working too young (yipping in frustration as the rabbit accelerates away from the immature dog) or working in woodland where the quarry can get through faster than the dog, which yips in exasperation. A noisy lurcher is a great irritation, but probably no more than that unless the owner is working in a place or at a time where it is better to be discreet. Even when working with full permission, there are places where passers-by can take it upon themselves to interfere, or at night where people can be over-fearful of noise outside. It also wastes breath that would be more usefully spent in running. It is better by far to research the lurcher's parentage so that you know she does not come from a family of yippers, to enter the dog when she is old and strong enough, and to keep the immature pup away from situations that will ask too much of her. Once yipping is established as a habit, it is impossible to eradicate.

However, one yap does not a yipper make. Young lurchers tend to be very vocal, with an engaging vocabulary of yowls and groans which they use in their everyday interaction with their owners. Early in a lurcher's education, she might moan softly with anticipation at the entrance to a rabbit bury, or mumble softly in the car when on the way to do something exciting (she knows it is going to be exciting – she has seen the ferrets and nets go in, or the lamp, and you are in your hunting clothes). Many young lurchers do this, but go on to be silent workers, so do not fret if your pup is one of the chatty sort. This is a world away from a barrage of yaps while on the scut of a fleeing rabbit.

Hard Mouth

Again, this is often inborn, though it can be acquired. Terrier crosses are particularly prone to hard mouth, but any sort of lurcher can be.

Hunting squirrels

There are degrees of hard mouth, too, from the shattered carcase in which every bone seems to have been crushed to the one bruised and maybe penetrated from a decisive strike. Whether hard mouth bothers you depends on the quarry that you hunt and what you do with it afterwards. Thus the person who expects to sell rabbits to the butcher or game dealer has a problem, whereas the one who uses rabbit meat to feed dogs and ferrets, hawks or snakes generally does not mind. Hunters of biting vermin, such as foxes, squirrels, mink and the like, need the dog to kill on pickup, whereas a deer carcase should be as near clean as possible (and a good lurcher will do that job better than a rifle). Hares struggle mightily when caught, and a dog soft-mouthed on rabbits will often kill hares to make the carry-back easier. Sometimes a dog will start to kill rabbits after it has had a raking from the hindlegs of one when retrieving, or even been bitten – I have been bitten by rabbits, and it is quite a bite. Hardmouth is common in dogs that have been consistently over-run, because a tired dog will strike rabbits with increasing desperation, and seek to immobilise them rather than carry them back alive.

I have known a number of dogs that catch a rabbit gently and then bite it once to kill it and stop it struggling, and also some that carry back right to hand and then kill the rabbit before handing it over. Dogs scored by pheasant spurs can turn hard-mouthed once they learn a squeeze to the ribcage stops all that nonsense. Many dogs have the wit to know which quarry needs killing and which doesn't, and to carry live quarry in such a way that it cannot hurt them. I had one that would fold pheasants neatly in her mouth, and carry rabbits back by their back skin. She was so soft-mouthed that every year a handful of rabbits would kick out of her mouth, but she was a demon on foxes and squirrels.

Is a hard mouth a real problem? I do not find it so. Those who need a soft-mouthed dog would be well advised to work theirs only on rabbits, not to enter them too young, and never to over-work them.

Jibbing

Jibbing, quitting or jacking mean the dog that either does not run the quarry at all if she does not want to, or runs it half-heartedly, breaking off from the chase when she would otherwise have had a good chance of catching. This last is critical: there are those who persistently send their dogs on impossible targets, which de-moralises the dogs and ruins their confidence. Running dogs are sensitive beasts, and are easily discouraged by this sort of foolishness. Unlike the previous faults mentioned, which can be inborn as well as acquired, the jibber is always a case of bad management. The dog may have been run too young, or too much, or when injured, unfit, or without due preparation (such as in the case of foxing). Otherwise, the dog may have been shouted at or punished if it did not catch. Whatever the background, the dog anticipates pain or fear from running the quarry, and so chooses not to. Dogs are great stoics about pain, and some owners do not give enough thought to physical stresses such as running a dog on difficult ground, or in the heat, with aching joints and muscles, or suffering from dehydration, cold or cramp. Lurchers are born with a passion for hunting, and the right owners nurture this to fruition, stifling the urge to run the dog when she either is not ready or has no hope of succeeding. A dog run near to peak fitness on quarry that she has every chance of catching will not become a quitter through missing some of the animals she runs, but instead will become keener. A dog that is thoroughly demoralised, exhausted or in pain, will sooner or later throw in the towel, no matter how game. Owning a quitter points the finger of accusation at the owner rather than the dog.

Time

Whether you have a young pup or you are making the best of a second-hand (or more) dog, you should not be so eager to get her working that you neglect these basics, for if you ever want to progress to advanced lurcher work, every brick must be in place straight or the whole edifice will come down. Time spent on all this is never time wasted. Patience, a sense of timing and a total lack of ego are vital attributes for the would-be lurcher owner. Let us see where you can go from here.

2 The Rabbiter's Dog

Ferrets, Nets, Lamps and Hedgerows

If ever there is a picture of the traditional lurcher, it is of the dog sloping along in the shadows with a rabbit in her mouth. Probably poached throughout the centuries more than any other animal in Britain, the rabbit lacks the feeding potential of the deer and the glamour of the hare, but it fits neatly up a sleeve, down a trouser leg (though it doesn't half itch when the fleas start to leave the carcase) or in a capacious pocket or curiously baggy coat lining. The rabbit could be picked up discreetly at dawn or dusk, easily hidden until a convenient time came along to remove it from a 'hot' area, and was quickly processed compared with other game, where feathers or big heads and legs could lead to difficulties. The poaching dog could jump out of a trap drawn by a pony (good view over the hedgerows from these) pick up a rabbit and be back in the

Lurcher in the shadows (*Phil Lloyd*)

46

vehicle hidden under a blanket before anyone could see. More modern dogs can be out of a motor vehicle and back with their illicit booty in much the same way, and when times were hard for me, I owned a useful lurcher who would snap rabbits up off the grass verge and be back in the car in a flash. Rabbits fed many a poor family, often being the only meat they saw from one month to the next, were easy to sell or barter, and up until relatively recently, the skins had as much value for the felt-making trade as the body had for meat.

Nowadays, farmers and other landowners are pleased for trustworthy people to help control their rabbits, and there is no need to poach, though old habits die hard in some people. Rabbits can be recycled as food for dogs, cats, ferrets, hawks and snakes as well as people. Rabbit meat is easily digested, and adapts to a huge variety of cooking methods, from traditional pies and stews to a more modern curry for the tough old buck. Young rabbits are still known as 'fryers' in some areas, tender little morsels to be fried in butter and served with a thick slice of bread to mop up the juices. Mouth watering yet?

The Sporting Rabbit

The rabbit is a vastly underrated quarry by those who have never hunted it, and I have seen some of the best dog work of my life while hunting rabbits. The rabbiting lurcher needs more in the way of skills and training than probably any other working dog of any kind, due as much to the many different methods we have of catching rabbits as the rabbits themselves. The 'small beast in hodden grey' is a master of survival, and it is a good dog that can find and take daytime rabbits consistently on different types of land. Rabbits are less difficult to catch in some parts of the country than in others, and a dog taking high numbers in one area may be pushed to pick up any at all elsewhere. As a generalisation, the south of England produces some of the most testing rabbiting, while the northernmost areas and Scotland are easier, but that is not to say that the rabbit is an easy quarry anywhere. Less experienced rabbiters will say that a rabbit is a rabbit wherever you hunt it, but that just exposes their lack of knowledge and is apt to make more experienced coneycatchers smile quietly to themselves. As with any prey species, the less rabbits are disturbed, the less wary they are, but they soon learn the signs of new dangers and it doesn't take them long to respond. The more different places that a rabbiting dog works, the better she gets, but there is always a rabbit that will make the best dog look an utter fool, and the best rabbiting men and women know to tip their hat to that rabbit in acknowledgement of its abilities, rather than be put out at their dog's apparent (and unexpected) lack of skill. There are numerous ways for a dog and human combination to catch rabbits, and in given situations some are better than others; the best dogs know them all. Whatever else you want your dog to do, you cannot beat a year's rabbiting as a starting point, for it will teach hunting skills in a way that other disciplines cannot better. How and in which order these skills are taught is a matter for the individual rabbiter, dog and tract of land.

Bushing

This is the art of finding, flushing and catching a rabbit that is lying above ground. Here, the dog works on her own initiative, though human help is appreciated in certain situations. Rabbits lie up in thick thorn cover, long grass, tussocks – anywhere that will conceal a rabbit, and believe me, it doesn't take much to hide a rabbit that doesn't want to be seen. The bushing dog needs to know how to use her nose to find a sitting rabbit, whether following a scent trail that might be hours old, or winding the rabbit as she passes its refuge.

Finding . . .

. . . and catching *(James Whiteman)*

. . . and retrieving *(Roly Boughton)*

The owner is alerted by the dog's body language as she becomes progressively more excited following the scent, or freezes on point as she marks the place where the rabbit is hidden. As she homes in on the rabbit scent, you will see her ears lifted to the point that they cover the top of her forehead – I call this her 'hunting hat' – and that

Sitting tightly

long tail will start to circle. A rabbit lying in the open – known as a 'sitter' or 'squatter' – may be lifted straight from its seat before it gets a chance to run, or else it might flush as the dog approaches, to be chased and either caught or lost. Rabbits deep in bramble bushes and the like will sit very tightly, and are often evicted only by the dog entering the cover, or the owner riddling the rabbit out with a stick. Beating the cover has little effect, as the rabbit will usually just hunch down further; much more success is achieved by poking the stick in at ground level. Some lurchers are exceptional cover-bashers, especially if they have terrier blood in them, but of course the dog working inside the thicket is not then in a position to course the bolting rabbit when it leaves. Rabbits seldom offer a long course, and even if your dog responds straight away to your holloa, the rabbit stands a better than average chance of getting away. This is a time when a second dog can be very useful: one to enter cover and one to course. Smart lurchers will learn to stand in the rabbit-run, that track beaten in the grass to show the rabbits' favoured line across to the next place of safety, and scoop the rabbit up as it leaves, and my old silver dog was still catching into her late teens simply by knowing the right place and being in it. Some lurchers will circle the cover, making feints into it, until the rabbit loses its nerve and bolts, and others will pinpoint the rabbit exactly, waiting for you to join in with your stick. Bushing is one area where you do not need to be quiet or worry about wind direction, as often just standing letting your scent blow into the cover can be sufficient to make the rabbit leave, human scent being far more unsettling to them than that of dog, fox or any other of their myriad predators. Sometimes rabbits sneak out long and low, rather than bolting, so everyone needs their wits about them. Few animals are quieter than a rabbit which does not want to be heard. Their feet are entirely covered in fur – you cannot see a rabbit's pads – and you will not hear a footstep, though once they are safe they will often thump a warning with their hindlegs.

Rabbits are very fast sprinters, and well capable of straightlining a fast dog over a short distance, as long as they know where they are going. A rabbit that is off its own territory is much easier for the dog to pick up. Rabbits will hesitate fractionally before they enter cover or go down a hole, through a fence or hedge, and that is where the dog has a chance of catching, but also where many dogs can be injured. Rabbits will run under farm machinery, buildings, vehicles, anywhere a rabbit will fit, and the dog running hard in its wake has a risk of collision, which is of course why rabbits do that. I have had dogs run into trees (concussion and dislocated shoulder) a pylon (severe bruising) and a cross-country fence (the rabbit miscalculated and broke its neck: the dog was concussed and bruised) and barbed-wire fences, and I have been lucky, for others have had dogs break their necks or backs hitting obstacles while pursuing rabbits. I had a lurcher whose speciality was snatching rabbits out of rabbit holes

Hiding in farm machinery

as they made a dash for refuge, and how she never broke her neck doing this is a mystery. She frequently somersaulted with the whole of her head down the rabbit hole, and there is a gamekeeper who talks about her to this day, having seen her in action on his shoot.

Because the rabbit is so small and therefore fits through such tiny gaps, dogs run far more risk of injury than when coursing larger or slower quarry. This is why it is so important for pups to be educated about obstacles long before they see and chase a rabbit, and well before they have grown into their full speed. Personally, I always check ground before I work it, letting the dogs nose round the obstacles so that they know where they are, and if there are particular hazards, such as rubbish tips full of broken glass and rusting metal, or the chain-harrows hidden in long grass, then I don't risk the dog at all. No rabbit is worth an injured dog.

Terrier and Lurchers

This might seem to be the ideal team, with the terrier bustling game out of cover, and the lurcher coursing it. If you don't get it right, though, it can mean the lurcher in the thicket and the terrier pelting fruitlessly and noisily after the rabbits. Brian Plummer, who kept packs of terriers and numerous lurchers in prime rabbiting country

Terriers and lurchers working together

would never work them together. If a lurcher makes a catch and is then harassed by one or more terriers trying to rip the rabbit out of her mouth as she retrieves it, this can spoil her retrieving very quickly and beyond saving. Lurchers can develop all sorts of evasive behaviours then, from running off with the rabbit to eating it. However, bushing is one of my favourite methods of rabbiting, and the way to do it properly is to train your terriers as well as your lurchers. Personally, I prefer to have someone else working the terriers while I concentrate on the lurchers. One of each works the best, though at one time I was running a pack of five lurchers with a friend's two terriers, and we certainly took some quarry. What you must have is terriers that come off the quarry as soon as it has left cover, so that the lurcher can course and retrieve un-impeded. It is perfectly possible to train terriers to this standard, and once it has been established, the terrier and lurcher mix will be a great success. Do not, however, risk your well-behaved dogs of either sort with a strange, unproven one that someone wants to bring along. A lurcher that dives onto a terrier can injure it or pre-cipitate a fight, into which all the other terriers are likely to join, and it doesn't take much for a terrier to ruin a sensitive lurcher. Furthermore, not only is the resulting rabbit unusable except for ferret food, the last minutes of its life could be very unpleasant, and this is not acceptable, no matter how much of a pest it may be.

By contrast, the trained terrier is as pleasant to have around as the trained lurcher. Terriers have excellent noses and a very economical method of working. They don't thrash and crash through cover in the manner of the more ebullient gundogs, but instead toddle purposefully along, within the cover or at the edge of it, until they detect a worthwhile scent. Then they slide deep into the thorn thicket, and your heart rate increases as you hear them crackling their way to their objective, until with a volley of yaps and a last crunching charge, they eject the rabbit, and your running dog launches in pursuit. Sometimes of course a rabbit will under-estimate the opposition and sit fatally too long. Then you will hear a crash and a squeal, a pause, and the terrier, if it has been well-trained, will retrieve the rabbit to its owner. Less obliging terriers specialise in the internal retrieve, possibly to be chundered up in the car later. You would be amazed at how much rabbit a small terrier can eat.

There are many joys to bushing. You can take out several dogs and not only have them working as a team, but including you in that team as an honorary dog. Each dog has its favourite task, and you can help with your stick, your superior vision from your greater height, and by carrying the rabbits. With other disciplines, more than one dog can be too many, but bushing is a very enjoyable way to exercise a pack of dogs and see good pest control as well. However, each dog must be disciplined to work to you as an individual before being allowed to work in a pack, or else you risk anarchy. As a way of seeing dog work at its purest, I find bushing very hard to beat.

Lamping

This is a relatively modern sport in that it had to wait for lamps to be invented, and really only took off in the late nineteen-seventies, when the rabbit population in the UK was recovering from the onslaught of myxomatosis in 1953 and thereafter. Early lamps were heavy and messy, involving car batteries and headlamps, and a certain amount of acid spillage down your back as you struggled through fences, weighed down with equipment. A decade later brought a plethora of smaller, neater batteries and lamping kits, and these have continued to improve, with a variety of different sorts available. I find the belt packs easiest to carry, as I am short and not particularly strong. However, to support a belt-pack you do need hips, and the more slender among us will find the addition of a diagonal shoulder-strap a great assistance. Lamps go up in power from around 250,000 to two million candlepower; for rabbiting I find 250,000 to 500,000 perfectly adequate. There is no point in illuminating further than the dog can run, or attracting any more attention than you need.

Weather

The ideal lamping night is overcast and windy, for then rabbits will find it more difficult to see and hear your approach. If, however, you only lamp on ideal nights, you will not get out all that often, so it is worth trying on the less-than-perfect night. The weather during the day can have a marked effect on whether or when the rabbits will be out feeding: a warm, bright afternoon will often have them fully fed and in bed early, whereas a wet day or a series of wet days will tempt them out to feed by night. Generally, you will find better results on a bright night than a still night, though you should allow for the wind carrying your scent. Equally, you will likely see more rabbits out if you lamp the latter part of the night rather than as soon as it gets dark, for the rabbits like to have one final feed before the dew starts.

Basics

Like many of life's better experiences, lamping is easy to do badly, and in some areas inept lamping and an average dog are still quite adequate to produce reasonable catches of rabbits. In others, you need a fair bit of fieldcraft and a very good dog. Rabbits learn very quickly that a lamp is bad news, and become lamp-shy, so that it is difficult to get close enough to them for a reasonable slip. The basics are straightforward enough: you enter the field, switch on the lamp, search for a rabbit, make sure that the dog has seen it, and send the dog after it. Keeping the rabbit in the beam, you watch the dog's pursuit and when it has caught or missed, you switch off the lamp, which is the dog's signal to return. Basic skills in the human side of the arrangement include being as quiet as possible, working with the contours of the land in the dog's favour, for dogs run better uphill than down, understanding that the dog, being shorter, has a far different field of vision and often cannot see the rabbit until it moves, working into the wind as much as you can (sometimes the topography doesn't allow this) and choosing each rabbit to give the dog the best chance of catching. Skills in the dog involve trusting the beam, boxing the rabbit away from refuge, putting sufficient pressure on it that it makes a mistake, effecting a neat pickup, and coming straight back, catch or miss. A lamping dog needs speed, the intelligence to read the quarry and stop it from

Lamping *(Phil Lloyd)*

going where it intends, drive to put pressure on it and not to quit when it runs into cover, for often the rabbit will come straight out again, strike to put an end to the course, and the obedience and willingness to deliver the rabbit straight back to hand, or if unsuccessful, to return to the owner's side instead of hunting on in the dark. Some dogs, instead of running down the beam, choose to run outside it and come into the rabbit out of the darkness, which can be very effective. The lamper should keep the beam on the rabbit not on the dog, and illuminate as little area as possible, taking care not to shine over the brow of a hill and give advance warning to the other rabbits.

There are parts of the country where rabbits are not disturbed all that much and so they tend to sit rather than run when they see a light. Dogs need to be trained to take sitters, for their eyesight is different from ours and they often cannot see them. Many people teach the dog a particular soft whistle to indicate that she should be looking on the ground where the pool of light ends. Some dogs never develop the knack, but most can be trained to it, and it is a golden moment when your lurcher picks her first sitter. However, pretty soon, those sitters have either been caught, or taught that sitting is not such a good plan, and then the rabbits will run as soon as they see a beam, or, in heavily lamped areas, as soon as they hear a vehicle engine being switched off. Then the lamper has to be a little

Obedient and willing *(Phil Lloyd)*

56

trigger-happy, getting the dog into a good place in the dark, and then switching on the lamp and slipping straight away.

The Slip

Ah yes, the slip. This is the method by which you keep the dog with you until you wish to send it. These can be as basic or as fancy as you wish, but to my mind, a slip should be easy to use and not harsh on the hand. I use a dog lead with the metal catch cut off, and thread it through the collar. Thus the dog can be sent with a soft command, the slip has no mechanism which might jam, and the lead does not blister you if it runs through your fingers. Night work is no place for the elaborate coursing slip, which is too much of a fiddle to re-attach each time in the dark. Much has been written about the virtues of working a dog off the slip, implying that those owners who use a slip are somehow inadequate. Whether or not you use a slip is between you and the dog: some dogs are so keen that a slip is always needed, and if you are lamping with friends then slips are, in my opinion, only polite. One dog to one rabbit is the proper way, for any more than that and there is risk of collision and injury. It is easy enough for a lamping dog to be injured: you don't have to go looking for trouble. For this reason, I don't want a dog to leap fences in pursuit in the dark, for you never know what hazards might lie concealed on the other side. When I cross an obstacle to go from field to field, I leave the dog in a 'wait' while I check the landing side is safe, and then signal it to come over, illuminating the landing side where I want the dog to jump. The dog should be trained to stop dead as soon as she has landed over the fence, so that she does not run into the field and startle the rabbits into running before the lamper is ready.

The Collar

Many people prefer to run their dogs without collars, as they fear that they might get caught up. Others feel that the collar gives a degree of protection, especially if you come across a fox, and the broad collar that is traditionally worn by running dogs was designed to protect the neck. I have never personally seen a dog caught up when running by night, and I do possess a collar with a fang-hole right through it, but this was a single occasion in many years of foxing. Once again, it is purely a matter of choice whether you run the dog with a collar on or not. However, if you do, remember to silence the identification disc with tape or a well-placed elastic band.

Filters

Some people like to use coloured filters over the lamp with the idea that rabbits will not be as spooked by a coloured light as by a white one. Scanning the field with the coloured light, they then change to the white light once they have chosen a rabbit to run. Red is the usual filter to use, though I do know people who use blue or green. Animals' eyes differ from our own in the way they see colour, though animals are not, as was once thought, colour blind. I find that rabbits quickly learn about coloured filters, though the first time or two that these are used they can give a reasonable advantage where rabbits have become lamp-shy to a white light. Personally, I find it much more difficult to see with a coloured filter, so I only ever use them when foxing. If you do fit coloured filters, be sure that you can flip them off and on silently, as rabbits react at once to unnatural sounds.

Tactics

Discipline is as tight with lamping as it is free with bushing. The lamping dog must work to the will of her handler, only chasing the rabbits chosen for her, and coming straight back after each one. It is useful if the dog knows to come off quarry and return as soon as the lamp is switched off, because you sometimes have other animals popping up in the beam when the dog is running. Likewise, however good your dog, you do not want her to decide which rabbits to chase. Some of them might be in an unsafe area that you know about and the dog doesn't, and some might not be rabbits at all.

It is important to walk your lamping ground in the daylight before you tackle it in the dark, so that you are aware of unsafe areas, bad ground and good places to cross boundaries. This also gives you a chance to check out the rabbit buries and runs so that you get some idea of where you will find rabbits and which way they will run. You need to know where the neighbours are, as people can get twitchy about lights shining near their houses at night, and you would be wise never to shine a lamp so that the light goes into a window.

Lamping styles vary, and it is good to go out with as many people as you can persuade to take you, to see the different methods in action. Some people only ever shine the lamp for the briefest of look-arounds while others tend to keep the beam on for longer; some rock the lamp to keep a sitting rabbit on its seat, and some find that this done very quickly can disconcert a rabbit that is approaching cover and make it hesitate. Some lamps will allow differently-sized beams, so a narrow one can be used for pinpointing the quarry, and the dog can be trained to go when the broad beam is switched on. Some swear by lamping where they have been and not where they are going, i.e. behind them not before, and others use the 'lighthouse' method of standing in one spot and sending the beam all around. I have even known people who, holding the lamp aloft, ran after the rabbit themselves, which requires a deal of agility not to mention plain luck in the dark, as it is so easy to catch your toe in a rut or twist an ankle. It is also pointless, as the dog runs so much better.

A rabbit that runs into cover will often pop out again if you keep the lamp on, and many a catch has been on the rebound, so to speak. Never be too idle to go into a field and try to lamp it from outside, for you are likely to be shown up as the rabbit comes into cover at an angle that you cannot follow, or else goes into some dead ground where the lamp cannot illuminate. The dog has to run, so you do your bit too and help as much as possible.

Learning Curve

Though some dogs are naturals at the lamping game, most have to learn the ways of the rabbit by night, and the catch rate may not be so good initially. Rabbits can turn and jink at top speed, leaving the dog sprawling in a tangle of legs until she learns to slow down in the stride that takes her up to the rabbit and to anticipate its evasive movements. I have seen rabbits leap clear over the top of a lurcher, landing running facing the other way. I have also seen lurchers wise to this making a huge leap and catching the rabbit in mid-air. Good dogs learn to box the rabbit away from cover and try to anticipate its manoeuvres, all the while running hard, and the astute owner will be aware of how unbalancing it can be to run at speed in the dark after a small agile quarry and then move the head sharply to catch. Many dogs somersault with the effort, which is heart-stopping to watch. Because quarry only runs as fast as it is pressed, a clever dog will keep speed in reserve and then accelerate into her rabbit, scooping it up before it has a chance to jink or even realise that it should. I used to lamp with a friend's very Greyhoundy lurcher, which would seldom get a turn out of a rabbit as he would

Rabbits turn and jink at top speed *(Phil Lloyd)*

be on them and pick up before the rabbit had even begun to realise it was in danger. However, he was clumsy on the turn, and if a rabbit did swerve, he would lose it.

Company

Lamping is one of those activities that is best done alone or with one companion. The more people involved, the more noise and scent they can produce, no matter how careful, and rabbits don't have those long ears and whiffly noses for nothing. Although I have known people lamp more than one dog each, it takes a fair amount of dexterity as well as training, or else causes even more noise as one dog struggles on the slip while the other is coursing. One friend used to leave one dog in the car while she lamped the other, changing dogs when she changed batteries, but each dog had to be caged and muzzled while left, and there is always a risk of theft when leaving a dog in a vehicle, even on private land. If you choose to do this, make sure that the dog in the vehicle has a coat on if it has run, and has been offered a drink. Two people each lamping with one dog can make quite a dent in rabbit populations, and it

Making a dent in the rabbit population *(Roly Boughton)*

61

makes for twice the fun as long as good manners are observed, which includes keeping one dog away from the action while the other is working, not slipping the second dog until the first is caught up, and making sure that collars, if worn, are tight enough not to slip over that snakelike head if a dog tends to get over-excited and struggle. A lurcher can back out of a collar faster than you would believe, and sometimes a controlling arm around the quarters is necessary. It is easier if each person does their own lamping, as it is surprisingly difficult to see the rabbit if you are not looking directly down the beam. Visitors should be properly briefed if they have never been lamping before, as I have known people try to trip the rabbit up as it passes them, which could have catastrophic consequences for the dog (or the outstretched leg) and even if no lasting damage is done, it can be the end of a beautiful friendship.

Lamping Types

While any size and type of lurcher will make a good bushing dog, the lamper's needs are more specific. In most areas, a fast dog is needed, one with at least fifty per cent sighthound in the mixture. I have read about purebred Border collies being successful lamping dogs, and all I can say is that it must be in remote, rabbit-infested areas, for I have tried to lamp with these and they are so slow that they can't get on terms with the rabbits at all. As well as being fast, the lamping dog should be agile. An ideal size is between 23 and 25 inches, for though smaller and larger dogs will make good lampers, they have to try a lot harder. Smaller dogs won't have the height advantage to see so far, and very tall ones are not so well placed for getting down to quarry as low to the ground as a running rabbit. Small dogs take their rabbit at a different angle from large dogs, reaching forward rather than down, and I remember one huge dog that used to trip the rabbit with his front feet and flick it into his jaws, a most amazing knack to witness. Some people need stamina in a lamping dog, but relatively few of us go on lamping all night these days, for you need a prodigious amount of ground to do so, not to mention a few slaves for carrying the rabbits. Two to four hours is enough for a hobby hunter like me, with other commitments during the day, for you have to deal with the catch once you get home as well. Thus a very sighthoundy dog will do the job just as well, having a fast recovery rate as well as a good turn of foot.

Slower, tougher dogs such as those with fifty per cent or less sighthound in them will still make good lampers in some areas, indeed they can be the best lampers where there are plenty of rabbits and the ground is rough, steep and rocky. There is a tendency in some types of collie cross to start picking and choosing which rabbits they will run after a season or two, or even if they will run at all, which can be annoying. If yours starts this, make sure that there is no physical reason why she won't run, and then try letting her watch another dog run. If that doesn't work, take her away from lamping for a while and then try her a few months later. Some will also attempt to stalk the rabbit in the beam rather than chasing it. This will still catch rabbits, though it is not as spectacular to watch as what one observer called 'The Waterloo Cup by moonlight' which is what delights so many about this branch of pest control. A dog that runs the beam can take two rabbits in the time that it takes the stalker to catch one, though of course you can argue that the slower dog is not taking so much out of itself. The stalking dog will only catch sitters, and rabbits will not sit once they have learned what the glare of the lamp means, so there are relatively few opportunities for the stalking dog. Personally, it would irritate the hell out of me to wait for a dog to stalk down the beam, but each to their own.

Some dedicated lampers keep their dogs only for lamping, and do not allow them to hunt by day, as they do not want a dog using its nose and running on in the dark. Most of us, however, need a dog with more than one string to its bow, and I have never personally owned a dog so stupid that it couldn't tell whether it was lamping or not. Though they may start with their noses on the ground, and may well hunt on initially, lurchers quickly catch on to the lamping discipline, watching the beam eagerly as the lamper searches for a suitable rabbit. Once a lurcher is trained to the lamp, handlers must be very careful that the dog does not try to follow other lights, car headlights for instance, which could take her into danger.

Strike

Large or small, fast or slow, what a lamping dog needs most of all is strike. Rabbits are seldom far from refuge, and the dog that doesn't know how to use her mouth will not get a second chance the way she will with some quarry. Strike is the action that picks up the rabbit, and some dogs strike like rattlesnakes. My fawn bitch was known as 'scissormouth' because once those long jaws opened, they seldom closed without fur or feather in them. Her granddaughter, just starting at the time of writing, strikes so hard that the rabbit is bruised at point of contact. As we use most of the rabbits we catch for dog and ferret food, this is not a problem to us, though of course it would not be acceptable in a butcher's rabbit. This pup does not kill her rabbits, and their skin is never pierced, but her

The strike *(Phil Lloyd)*

strike is awesome, and a rabbit does not go anywhere once she has made contact. Strike should not be confused with hard mouth, which is when the dog bites into the rabbit, piercing the flesh and sometimes crunching the bone. Strike is definitely inherited: hard mouth often is, but it is also easy to make a dog hard-mouthed through working her too hard too young. You cannot teach a dog strike: it is either there or not. Nor can you tell if she will have it until she starts hunting properly, for some dogs are slow to start using their mouths, often trying to trap the rabbit with their paws when they start.

Lamping is hard on a dog, and most will be past their best at an age where there is still plenty of other work that they can do. Personally, I have never lamped a rabbit dog past nine years old, but I do live in an area where lamping dogs need a lot of speed, and they have to work very hard for every rabbit they catch.

Aftercare
Once you have finished your night's activities, the dog should be offered a small drink, preferably with electrolytes in it or else honey and salt mixed into it at the ratio of one teaspoon of each to one pint. Always carry a flask of hot water, some of which can be used to take the chill off the drink, and which otherwise may be a blessing in case of needing to wash an injury, when you would dilute it to a suitable

temperature with the cold water that should always be carried in the vehicle when out with a dog. A first-aid kit is a sensible precaution, too, as well as a blanket if you need to transport an immobile dog or wrap up a sick one. Assuming no injury, the dog would be glad of a coat in colder weather for the journey home, for she can lose a lot of weight in a few hours of lamping, and her muscles will benefit from not being allowed to get chilled after exertion. This is nothing to do with making a dog 'soft' and everything to do with keeping her healthy. Once home, the dog can be allowed to drink deeply while you check her over for cuts and scrapes, being especially thorough with her feet and nails. A lot of people bathe the feet and scrub off excess mud with an old toothbrush. Salt water is better used than adding disinfectant, as not all of the latter are dog-friendly, and the dog might lick her paws afterwards.

Then give the dog a light meal and leave her to sleep, offering the main meal after she has rested. If the dog is not interested in food and sleeps unusually deeply, then she has overdone it and should be rested until she is back to her normal self. Every other night is plenty for a lamping dog, and if that is what you do, it is unreasonable to expect her to go ferreting on the days between.

Nights Without Lights

As dogs' night vision is far better than ours, they are perfectly capable of catching game without our using a lamp. To be honest, the lamp does not assist them all that much once the rabbit is on the run, particularly if the lamper is not sufficiently on the ball to keep the lamp on the rabbit, or to back up and turn quickly so that the light is not directly in the dog's eyes if the rabbit chooses to run straight at the lamper. Plenty of stories exist from pre-lamping days of dogs that were just loosed from their pens at night and which returned with the family's dinner in their jaws, and while no doubt many of these tales are fanciful, others are likely to have been true at least some of the time. Even nowadays, most lurcher owners have had dogs run off into the dark and come back with a rabbit. However, this is not the safest way to work your dog, especially if she is fast, for she is that much more at risk from collisions in the dark, and you might well not be able to find her just when she needs you most.

Doubling-Up

Don't. Two dogs run together on a rabbit will sooner or later run into each other, with the potential of causing injury or even death. One rabbit, one dog is the proper way, safe and sporting.

Long-Netting

This is supposedly a traditional lurcher skill which, I suspect, has virtually died out except as a novelty. Although people do still long-net rabbits at night, they mainly do so without a dog because, bluntly, a dog is not the best way of doing it, and a night-netting dog needs a degree of natural inclination as well as training. What is supposed to happen is that, on a suitable dark and windy night, the long-net is set, and then the dog is sent alone to herd the rabbits into the net but not attempt to catch them. Dogs with a large amount of herding blood would be the ones to use, even pure herding dogs, but unless they are working sheep and cattle during the day, or you do a powerful amount of long-netting, you are likely to be keeping a specialist dog for a job that it won't be doing all that much. In the old days, a dog was said sometimes to have a light attached to its collar to help send the rabbits in, but I am rather sceptical about that, too. Whereas nowadays it would be an easy matter to attach a small light to a dog's collar or even use one of the LED crystal collars you can buy from a pet shop, in the old poaching days when this practice was supposed to be rife, you would be talking about an enclosed candle or some sort of tiny lantern. However, assuming the dog's instinct was to herd rather

A good ferreting lurcher

than chase, it would have to put sufficient pressure on the rabbits to make them run into the net without seeing it, have the nous to leap or swerve off the net when close in, and resist catching any rabbit entangled, all without putting its light out or setting itself on fire. These requirements are not impossible by any means, but would not be readily found, I suspect. In all the years I have been watching lurchers work, I have never come across anybody who could demonstrate such a dog in action, nor have I ever heard of one that could unless it was a long time ago and conveniently since deceased. However, I know a tidy number of long-netters, all of whom favour a human colleague to walk the rabbits into the net. Some say that this person should shake a matchbox to make the rabbits run, others that a device known as a 'dead dog' or 'dumb dog' be used, which is a rope dragged along the ground between two people, and some that the noise of walking is quite enough to move the rabbits. It would be quite plausible to acquire a suitably-bred dog and train it to the night long-net, but I suspect that an awful lot of rabbits would be lost along the way, and it might not be all that good for the long-net either.

Gate-Nets

A variation on the theme is gate-netting, where a field gate is netted in such a way that a rabbit running beneath it is trapped in the net. The dog's part is to herd the rabbits into the gate-net in a similar way to the long-net, though the gate-net can be used more effectively by day than the long-net because it isn't so readily seen. Weighted with stones, it lies along one of the horizontal bars of the gate (or over it if the gate is metal) and has sufficient bag or 'kill' at the bottom to enmesh whatever runs into it. Rabbits will indeed run under gates quite readily, especially if pursued, and the astute gate-netter will pick places where there are signs to show that the rabbits already run under the gate as a matter of course. It isn't a disaster if the dog picks up the rabbit on its way to the net, either. Of course, you will need a powerful lot of gates and a decent rabbit population to catch many by gate-netting, and apart from the novelty, might conclude that there are better ways. The gate-net was once much used for catching hares, which is its true value because you get more meat for your efforts, and a slow dog will be just as useful as a fast one in that while you need a fast dog to catch a hare, a slower one can still put enough pressure on it to send it under a gate.

Holding a rabbit in the net (*Rob Moore*)

Ferreting

The ferreting lurcher is a highly-skilled dog, and a real pleasure to watch in action. Working totally on her own initiative, she indicates to the human side of the partnership which buries are occupied, holds or leaves rabbits in the net according to her owner's wishes, captures rabbits as they leave the bury before they have the chance to run, and is capable of coursing, catching and retrieving a rabbit that bolts and makes for another refuge. She ignores the rabbits once they are dead, is gentle with the ferrets, and some will even indicate where the ferret is underground if it has lain-up. A well-trained ferreting dog will enable a solo ferreter to cover both sides of a hedge, ditch or bank, and can literally double the catch, being even better than another human helper. Ferreting without a dog is like eggs without bacon; I have tackled such jobs where a dog would not be safe, such as beside a road or railway line, but there is little enjoyment in it compared to ferreting with a dog. In a suitable place, the

Catching in the mouth of the bury

addition of a dog makes the task a pleasure. Not only is the work done better and faster, you have the best of company and someone to help out with your lunch.

Marking

In a ferreting context, this means the dog shows the ferreter which buries have rabbits within. It is a common mistake to think that every rabbit hole has a rabbit in it, but rabbits don't live like that. Though an experienced ferreter can take an educated guess on whether a bury is occupied, a dog knows by use of its scenting abilities, and will show anyone who cares to understand simply by using body language. Some dogs mark more obviously than others, and will stand looking into the rabbit hole, often with one front paw raised in classic stance. Others will just glance at you quickly and look away, and you'd better be quick on the uptake to catch it. Many dogs mark subtly to start with and then, as their experience and confidence increases, you will get a more decisive mark. Marking is not just the prerequisite of the hunting dog: any dog will mark, given the opportunity. It requires skill on the part of the handler to understand the mark of any particular dog, and some very

Classic stance

experienced dogs will use slightly different body signals to indicate whether there is one rabbit or many rabbits, and whether they are deep in the bury or near the surface and ready to bolt. Rabbit smell is rabbit smell to us, but to animals, each one smells different, just as people look different to us. I have known rabbits so jumpy that they bolt as soon as I start setting the nets, and the dog will often be at hand to lift them as they do so. Walking to the buries, the astute ferreter watches the dog the whole time. The dog may follow scent to the bury and then mark ('One in here, Boss') or push out rabbits that have been feeding above ground and which will then run to the nearest refuge, if the dog does not succeed in picking them up en route. But if that rabbit doesn't live down that particular rabbit-hole, the rabbits that do will chase it around until it either comes out again, or else hides in a far corner of the bury. Rabbits are very territorial, which can be used to the hunter's advantage. Once while out night-shooting, I saw a mortally hit rabbit run down a rabbit-hole. Damn, I thought, lost that one. As I thought it, the rabbit bolted out of the rabbit-hole again, ran towards me and expired at my feet, having been ejected by the resident rabbits who had no intention of sharing their home with a stranger, especially one that was about to die and so foul their burrow.

False Mark
Dogs are not inclined to false mark by nature, but it is easy accidentally to train them to do so. False mark is when the dog marks an empty bury. Dogs should not be praised for marking, nor should

they be encouraged to mark. Instead, the mark should be rewarded by putting a ferret down the rabbit hole, and hoping that it will then bolt a rabbit. Of course, you will often see your dog marking rabbit holes when you are not out ferreting, especially once she has been ferreting and had her reward in the shape of a run on a bolting rabbit. Equally, and most frustratingly, it always seems to be when you have a young dog just learning, that the rabbits refuse to bolt, and the dog becomes bored waiting at the bury. However, a very important part of the psychology of any hunting animal is that it comes ready programmed to 'abort the mission' and is thus tolerant of failure providing some success is achieved at times. This characteristic exists because a predator that is injured is likely to starve to death, and so when a hunting situation becomes fruitless, the dog will be mentally attuned to leaving it and still be willing to try elsewhere. Constant failure without any success will put the dog off trying, and this too is a survival technique because it saves wasting precious energy on lost causes. Thus while training, you should do everything that you can to ensure success, but you do have a little leeway for when things go wrong – as they certainly will from time to time.

So, to recap – the dog marks as a matter of natural inclination every time she comes across an inhabited bury. Once she has learned that the mark is followed by a bolted rabbit, she will mark much more readily and decisively, but she will not stop marking if she does not get rewarded by having a rabbit to chase, any more than she will stop sniffing around when she is taken out, in the hope of finding scent to follow. All types of pet dogs that have never been worked and never will be, still mark, and most of the time the owner has not a clue what the dog is doing. So failing to reward the mark does not stop the dog marking, but rewarding the mark correctly by arranging a rabbit to appear will reinforce the marking behaviour. Encouraging the dog to display marking behaviour by praising her or egging her on at every bury will, however, cause the dog to false mark, because she has produced a natural behaviour which has pleased her owner, and therefore tries to please him or her again, because she associates approval with the act of marking.

There is one circumstance in which even the most reliable dog will appear to false mark, and that is when fresh rabbit scent goes into the bury, but the rabbit has left the bury immediately afterwards. You will sometimes see this in cover as well, when a rabbit has run through and out again without pausing. Understand your dog in this: she is working by scent and has marked correctly, because you only get this sort of mark where a rabbit has run into the bury just ahead of the dog. The dog has no way of telling that the rabbit has not lingered until the fresh scent starts to dissipate, or else when she scents the rabbit's exit point, when her demeanour will change enough for the astute handler to read what has happened. I once knew a very good dog put out of a prestigious Field Trial precisely this way, which did not reflect well on that judge's working experience. Dog and owner produced a blinding performance the following year, which I believe was some consolation.

Early Days

Starting a dog off ferreting means that rabbits will be lost in the initial stages while the dog organises her mouth and legs. I prefer to leave the majority of rabbit holes un-netted, so that the dog gets the chance to chase, which is a big reward whether or not she catches the rabbit. The discipline here is that the dog returns at once to the bury, catch or miss, and it takes a while for some dogs to learn to resist the allure of hunting on after a miss. Patience in the early stages is soon rewarded as the youngster calms down and becomes more sensible. I do not like to start a dog ferreting too young because

A first retrieve on the real thing (*Mike Bridle*)

of this need to steady down, but others take them ferreting while they are still measuring their age in weeks. It is more than likely that the tiny pup will pull nets about, get underfoot, get bored and wander off, or get cold, hungry and miserable. So long as you are patient, and prepared to pack up before the pup has lost interest, it doesn't really matter how soon you start it, but I like them to be at a stage where they can actually catch rabbits as this encourages them to do things my way.

Purse Nets
This is the most popular method of ferreting, where a net is placed over each rabbit hole before the ferrets are entered. There are several types of purse net, and everyone has their own favourites. From the lurcher point of view, there is only one area of dispute, though, and this is whether you want the dog to leave netted rabbits alone, or else pin them in the nets until you can get to them. This is a matter for the individual ferreter. I need a dog to hold rabbits in the net, because that way I don't get rabbits kicking their way out of the net before I can despatch them. Purse-netted rabbits really ping about, and it is a source of wonder to me that a small ferret can pull the net about every which way when going through the mesh, and yet a

Picking up a netted rabbit

rabbit many times larger can blast through the net with only a short delay. This is of course because the net is loose when the ferret goes through it, and the rabbit's struggles pull the net taut and enable it to get through. This is worth remembering when you pick up a netted rabbit – always pick up the rabbit not the net, or you will be left looking nonplussed as bunny slides through the net and away. When the dog gets there first, she is meant to hold the rabbit gently so that the net is not torn, nor the rabbit injured. Most pin the rabbit with their jaws, though a few, especially those with a large amount of collie in their makeup, will use their paws. So long as the rabbit is held securely, it doesn't matter which they do. I have owned one dog that killed rabbits in the net, which was not what I wanted, but he did not damage the nets and the rabbits certainly did not get away. We all have to compromise here and there, and it wasn't long after his dam retired before his daughter grew into a ferreting dog that was more to my taste, and he could concentrate on his preferred quarry, which was mainly fox, and small vermin on the side. Some say that using a rabbit dog on biting quarry will make it hard-mouthed on rabbits, but this isn't necessarily so: the only hard-mouthed dog I have owned was like that from the beginning and nothing ever got out of his mouth alive. Most of my others were soft-mouthed on rabbits no matter what else they caught.

Stop-Nets and Long-Nets

For daytime work, the only difference between these is their length. Some buries just cannot be purse-netted, such as those in thick cover where the ferreter cannot get to all the rabbit holes. Buries out in the open can be encircled by one or more nets; large buries can be divided into manageable sections with well-placed stop-nets, and known rabbit-runs along hedges and ditches will yield good results from a net across them. More accessible rabbit-holes can be either purse-netted or left open. Some ferreters prefer to use long-nets the whole time, for it is quicker to run out one or two 'webs' than to purse-net every rabbit hole. Success depends on the rabbits having read the book, however, for often they will just hop from rabbit-hole to rabbit-hole rather than bolt from the bury into the net. A trained dog over the bury can scoop up rabbits as they exit, or if they miss one, put it under sufficient pressure that it chooses to run to the next point of refuge rather than go back into the bury. The dog in pursuit must be trained not to hit the net after the rabbit, but either to leap the net and pin the rabbit from the other side, or else leave it completely. Long-nets need a good deal of bag or 'kill' at the bottom in order to enmesh the rabbit, otherwise bunny will bounce off the net to safety. Several rabbits in the net at once may pull the top-line

74

The long-net for daytime ferreting

down so that others just bound over the top, so in these cases, the dog is invaluable.

Long-nets are easier to use in areas where there is little to be caught up in them in the way of sticks, thorns and general woodland brash, otherwise you will spend what seems like half of your ferreting day unpicking bits of countryside from them. It is straightforward to train a lurcher to ferret with these nets: they almost always get entangled once and bring the whole lot down, but they are dogs that are acutely aware of their own embarrassment, and few will do that a second time. I train mine to the nets before we ever take the nets ferreting, so that they know to jump them, to leave a dummy thrown into the net and to retrieve one thrown over it.

No Nets

A really experienced dog will catch ferreted rabbits without the aid of nets at all. This is pure sport, for you will miss rabbits when several bolt at once, but it is marvellous dog work. The dog freezes above the bury, ears flicking as she follows the underground chase between ferrets and rabbits, picking up the sounds, and also feeling vibrations through her feet. Then she will lunge, and be standing there with a rabbit in her mouth, making it look easy. At first, a dog will push her head down the rabbit hole and stop the rabbit bolting: this is part of her learning, and mistakes have to be made. Soon the predator in her will tell her to wait clear of the entrances, and pounce

Working without nets

as the rabbit leaves. When rabbits creep out slowly, the dog will remain motionless until the rabbit is clear of the bury, then strike. I watched a ten-month-old pup do this recently on her very first outing with the ferrets; she is a flighty beast, and I never expected her to have such prey-sense so young. Surely the lurcher is the ultimate hunting dog.

Lurchers that learn this skill of sweeping up rabbits as they leave the bury can carry on working into their dotage, and can also fill the bag with relatively little physical effort, though the level of concentration should not be underestimated. I remember a most exasperating day's ferreting which was saved from total disaster by my fawn bitch's skill when we moved onto the final bury which was on the bank of a rife (huge drainage ditch to cope with tidal rivers). We had permission on one side but not the other, and so tired were we after a morning where everything had gone wrong, including my ferreting colleague falling into the rife, that we just ran the ferrets through and let the dogs work. My friend's Border collie turned the bolters towards my lurcher, and she in her turn scooped up rabbit after rabbit straight out of the rabbit holes. We caught twenty-two rabbits in just over an hour, which is astonishing for that kind of landscape. The landowner was unimpressed, however, as he'd seen 'at least thirty' rabbits on the bank the previous day.

Lurcher pup with ferret kits

Ferrets

We cannot leave ferreting without a word about the ferrets them-selves, and their working relationship with the lurcher. The traditional way to keep ferrets and lurchers on good terms was to feed puppies and ferret kits from the same bowl of milk so that they were used to each other from an early age. This comes from the days when everyone who worked ferrets and lurchers bred a litter of each every year. Times change, and we are much more careful with our breeding nowadays: I know dedicated ferreters and lurcher workers who have never bred from any of their animals, and as a consequence rarely have ferret kits and a puppy around at the same time. Lurchers being amiable beasts, it is easy to train them at any age not to harm ferrets, but I have never succeeded in teaching ferrets not to upset the dog. As even the smallest retaliatory nip from a lurcher could mean curtains for the ferret, I keep a very careful eye on each when I am working them together. Ferrets can get very fired-up when working, and although many are easy to handle whatever the circumstances, you will always get the odd one that you cannot trust. I have been lucky with mine, and only a few weeks ago my apprentice lurcher pulled a rabbit out of the bury with the ferret still attached. The sapling was horrified and dropped the rabbit, luckily close enough for me to grab; the ferret accepted her

Rabbit with ferret still attached *(Phil Lloyd)*

squirming apology and sniffed noses perfectly amiably before checking over the (now dead) rabbit for signs of activity and then going back down the bury. Had it gone otherwise, a bite from the ferret could have had a lasting detrimental effect on that young dog's future work.

Doubled-Up

There is quite a fashion at time of writing for working two lurchers over a rabbit bury when ferreting. Whether or not this is successful depends very much upon the dogs concerned, and the best result seems to be from using pairs of herding-dog crosses. I'll be the first to say that it would not work with mine as I use fast, very sighthoundy dogs that are jealous of their work and will not tolerate other dogs anywhere near the bury. The only exception was my fawn bitch and the Border collie ferreting as described earlier, and the only reason that this succeeded was because the collie deferred to her and pushed rabbits her way for her to course. She would only ever tolerate this one dog on the buries with her. You might think that one dog either side of a hedge or fence would be useful, but what tends to happen in practice is that you get both dogs on whichever side the first rabbits bolt, and then lose quarry from the

78

unguarded other side. One dog is perfectly adequate as a working partner with ferrets, but if you want to try them doubled-up, there is far less risk of injury than with lamping.

Many lurcher owners never look any further than the rabbit for their main, or even their only quarry. A good rabbiting lurcher will give years of service, and many unbeatable memories. While other quarry might seem more glamorous, there is no denying that the rabbit tests the lurcher thoroughly, and indeed the rabbiter too, and it is a good lurcher by any standards that can fill the freezer with rabbits.

3 The Foxing Lurcher

By Day and Night

Foxing lurchers are born, not made. If the dog doesn't have the inborn desire to connect with and despatch a fox, no amount of rearing and training will put it there.

Types

Your best bet for an out-and-out foxing lurcher is to buy a pup from proven parents, and if the breeder has bred several generations of foxers from his or her stock, all the better. Some crosses are more likely to take fox than others: Deerhound, Saluki and terrier composites tend to make good fox dogs, most Greyhounds will take them eagerly, and so will Whippets, their only disadvantage being their small size, easily overcome by crossing into larger types. Many

Bred from generations of foxing lurchers

Foxhounds

Whippets have the knack of despatching foxes without injury to themselves, but others are so fiery that caution is cast to the winds and they get injured. Thin Whippet skin tears so easily that some foxing Whippets look as if they have been duelling in Heidelberg, which can cause the odd raised eyebrow from outsiders. The great value of Whippet crossed into any lurcher mix is 'fire', that wonderful quality that has any fox dog fully committed to its quarry, and to ending the encounter as soon as possible.

You might think that Foxhound would be an ideal ingredient in a foxing lurcher, but it most definitely is not. To start with, the work of a Foxhound is a world away from that of a running dog, for although a Foxhound is fast, has stamina, and an inbuilt desire to hunt foxes, it does so by scent and as part of a pack, and most usually over a long distance. The voice of a Foxhound is part of its virtue, whereas we want our lurchers to be silent. Most crucially, and not generally known by those who have not been involved in the day-to-day aspects of a pack of hounds, is that not every Foxhound is willing to kill the fox. This is a specialised job within the pack, just as drawing, finding and following scent in different conditions are greater or lesser talents in different Foxhounds. They are truly marvellous animals, but their job is different, and they are not a good option to use in a lurcher.

Having acquired the raw material, it is still possible to ruin the dog for fox work by clumsy or premature entering: though some dogs will overcome inept handling, more will not and it is the easiest thing in the world to put a dog off this particular quarry. This is not

Long teeth

because (as some experts have suggested) the dog has no innate desire to take foxes. All dogs have a tremendous natural antipathy to foxes. However, the fox is no sinecure as a quarry. Not only are foxes surprisingly fast, they are as agile as a rabbit or hare, can turn every bit as quickly, and are experts in using every inch and contour of the land to throw off their pursuers. Moreover, and crucially, they can pack a bite out of all proportion to their size. Foxes have disproportionately long teeth in their long jaws, keep their heads in a crisis, and sell their lives dearly. If the dog does not have the knack of taking and despatching the fox cleanly and quickly, she will get bitten, and some dogs turn off very quickly once this has happened. Though there are collie (Border, Beardie and Border x Beardie) crosses, and indeed the occasional purebred Border collie that will hunt down and kill foxes, the collie cross is the least likely to make a committed fox killer unless the cur element is leavened by fifty per cent or more running dog. However, if collie lurchers are what suits you, pick a pup from a litter where both parents are proven foxers. I have seen some very able collie crosses take fox, so it can be done, though the downside of this particular breeding is that it frequently results in a dog that is touchy with other dogs as well. Whereas most sighthound mixes are gentle, affable souls when not actually dealing with their fox, the collie-bred fox killer can sometimes have collie surliness in its makeup, which the astute owner will allow for.

Deerhound and Saluki types are known for keeping their heads under pressure, and these dogs are both physically and mentally equipped to deal with biting quarry without getting hurt themselves. One of my best fox dogs, who caught a huge number of foxes in her life, only ever got bitten five times, each time when she was hampered from her killing strike by another dog. She caught her last fox just before her death at almost thirteen, and she was pure sighthound bred with no base blood at all. Terrier crosses, the most frequently used of which are Bedlington and Bull, don't care whether they get bitten or not, there being something in the terrier psyche that seems to react to this with a huge flush of endorphins and a powerful desire to bite back harder. The drawback with these is that once their dander is up, it takes a while for it to go back down again, and you have a dog that is so fired up that it can hold up your

Ragging the carcase

day's or night's work waiting for the dog to rejoin the normal world. I have more than once missed a second fox because my Bedlington cross has been ragging the carcase of the first, and dogs that do this take a lot out of themselves in the process. However, I love fire in dogs above many traits, and if that is how he gets his reward then who am I to deny him that pleasure? So long as the kill is quick, what happens to the cadaver is of no consequence unless you want the pelt. There is no market for these at time of writing, though there was one big black dog fox that I would dearly have liked to have taken to the taxidermist. Each hair on his body was russet tipped with black, and his legs were jet black, so that he looked pure black as he ran, and for several years we found red foxes with black brushes and a black stripe down their backs in that area, though no other that appeared completely black.

Skills

Best to have is the dog that takes her fox without getting bitten at all, or as near to that as possible. What size should a fox dog be? Ideally, big enough to lift the fox clear of the ground to shake it, but not so big that she loses turning ability. Some very large dogs can be extremely quick on their feet, and a narrow-bodied Deerhound type will often make a better foxer than a shorter but boxier type: it is a common mistake to think that 'large' invariably equals 'clumsy'. The Deerhound stride and long neck reach can take her right up to her fox to pick up and flick like a whip, and the fox has more to do to evade such a dog than it has with a shorter-striding one. Small dogs will take their fox at a different angle, which can leave them more vulnerable to a bite if they are thrown off their strike. Though smaller dogs can make formidable foxers, a good average size to aim for is twenty-four or twenty-five inches. Don't be concerned if your dog matures to either side of this, though, because the most important attribute of a fox dog is the desire to do the job.

You most particularly do not need aggression in a fox dog – or any type of hunting dog, for that matter. There is a world of difference between an animal with high prey drive, and one that is spoiling for a fight. To accelerate into a fox and take it decisively needs a cool head, sense, accuracy and timing. There is no room for foolhardy rashness in a dog that is going to make this her career. I have had dogs so nesh that they would cry if they trod on a nettle, but they made formidable foxers. How much excitement they show after they have killed their fox is neither here nor there, but they must keep their heads until then.

A clean, instant kill

I like a fast dog for fox work. Quarry of any sort only runs as hard as it is pressed, so those who have never seen a fox with a fast dog in pursuit may assume that foxes are not particularly swift runners. Nothing could be further from the truth, and a fox with a speed-merchant of a dog behind it doesn't half shift! Though slow dogs can catch foxes almost as well as faster ones, the crucial difference is in the amount of pressure put on the fox during the short sprint before it is caught. Going at full pelt takes a lot out of the fox, and makes for an easier pickup when the lurcher closes with it, and also gives the fox less time to think. The fox has lost much more of its breath and therefore its fight if run at 30 m.p.h. over fifty yards than at 10 m.p.h. for a hundred, and the fast lurcher still has enough in the tank to charge into her quarry, pick it up and shake it with that spine-dislocating wrench allied to the shock of sudden deceleration

Waiting for the bolt – two Deerhound lurchers

as she swerves and slides to a halt. Foxes do not generally know anything after that.

The other attribute I like in a fox dog is a good nose. Though foxes can be pungent beasts for much of the time, a fox resting in covert gives off little scent, and it takes a dog with a good nose to find the exact spot where one is lying-up. My Bedlington cross is an artist at this, and it is a keen delight to watch him circle a huge, thick patch of brambles that you'd think a rabbit would have trouble pene-trating, testing the air until he is sure of where his fox is. Then with a sudden rush, he smashes his way in, and is straight onto his target before it has time to uncurl. Nose is vital for all-round fox work, although if you only lamp your foxes, you will not need it in any great degree.

Preparation

The first couple of years of a foxing dog's life should be spent away from foxes. Basic obedience is necessary whatever you hunt, and then the dog needs at least a year of tackling rabbits, with other quarry as an optional extra. The great value of the rabbit is its sprinting speed and tremendous agility, allied to its size. The target is small, fast, can turn and jink at full speed, and is apt to vanish

Pup with fox brush

underground or into cover within a very short distance. Thus the dog learns to put in maximum effort from the first leap, to expect feints and sudden evasive manoeuvres as she closes for the pickup, and most of all, she will learn to strike. Dogs used mainly or solely on hares can lack that decisive strike because they know that they can afford to wait and get on terms with their hare, but there is no such luxury with a rabbit. Nor is there with a fox, which should not be taken half-heartedly, or allowed to get the upper hand in the chase. A dog which has served an apprenticeship on rabbits is far better equipped to make a sound fox dog than one which has not, though some people keep their dogs away from rabbits under the mistaken impression that it will make them unsteady. To a proven fox dog, rabbits are an *hors d'oeuvre*, and while they will go rabbiting quite cheerfully, there isn't a one that won't come off a fleeing rabbit to tackle a fox if one presents itself. I know people who set great store by bringing fox carcases home for the pup to rag, or letting her watch at a dig and then have a 'worry' of a warm cadaver, but none of that is necessary, nor is taking the pup to fox earths and hissing 'fox' at it. A dog that has never seen a fox before will go straight into it, if she is made of the right stuff. However, greater care is needed with entering to fox than to other quarry.

Entering

What you are wanting to ask me is why wait until the dog is two years old? No doubt you know dogs that have taken their first fox much earlier – and so do I. While some of these have gone on to make excellent foxers, more have quit and been sold on as rabbit dogs, and it is commonplace to find dogs that have gone cold on foxes at the same age that I start mine. You see, a sapling lurcher may look grown-up, but like any teenager, her body is constantly changing. Her proportions and her centre of gravity, her strength and her hormones will not have settled into their adult mode. This does not just apply to bitches, who of course have the hurdle of their first season to overcome as well, but to dog pups too. Because of the extra testosterone, male saplings will muscle up and look capable far earlier than bitches, but as in most creatures, the female is deadlier once she hits her form. Male dogs, as a rule (and acknowledging that all rules have exceptions) are just that little bit more nesh, and so need to be given every assistance at the beginning. That means waiting until they have learned to balance their bodies at all paces, to run and turn and strike, and – very important – to have tasted success. Then there is mental strength, which again only comes with maturity. Most well-socialised lurcher pups are naturally submissive to adult canids, and some of this can spill over into uncertainty with quarry that is perfectly prepared to face them down. Not just lurchers either: I once saw a fox challenge a group of three sapling Foxhounds and so psyche them out that it was able to walk through them to safety. Not just foxes, either, for I have seen a particularly feisty doe rabbit put a young terrier to flight.

For the sake of waiting a few months, your sapling dog can progress through this phase – which is natural and necessary, and prevents a pup from taking on more than she can manage – and become more assertive as she grows. Between her first and second birthdays, you will see her gradually coming into her own, and starting to stand up for herself with other dogs, and maybe developing something of a guarding instinct around you and the home. The precise time is different with each dog, but you will see the change in her, notice her developing character, and know when she is ready. A dog needs to go into a fox with confidence, and the first time, everything should go right.

Creating Success

I prefer to enter my own dogs to fox with a made dog. This way, they pick up from the other dog that this is a quarry to be given extra respect, and to be despatched with vigour, unlike a rabbit which can be retrieved unharmed. After this, I expect the dog to take foxes solo. This is because, though it is easier for two dogs to catch a fox, it is easier for a single dog to kill a fox, as it is crucial to a good kill for the dog to be able to lift the fox and shake it as well as deliver that shattering first bite. The shaking action dislocates the spine. With two dogs together, if they both go in for the kill, the fox cannot receive that shake, and the second dog to tackle the quarry stands a chance of being bitten. The fox hangs on when it bites, and if one dog is held and the other is trying to lift the fox, the bitten dog will be hurt further, and the fox will not have as quick a death, though it will still be a matter of only a few seconds. Sometimes a fox will lock its jaws in death, and then you still have to release its grip on the bitten dog. If, however, you use a two-dog team regularly, you can have suitable results if one dog will course but not tackle the fox, and the other will. I worked a dog-and-bitch team like this with great success, the bigger, faster dog putting real pace and pressure on the fox and the smaller bitch stripping turns out of it until she closed for the kill, which would be instant every time. These two would hem the fox in and stop it getting away, working it between

Fox

them at tremendous speed – for the bitch was no slouch – and from view to kill would be a matter of seconds. The bitch would flush from cover, and the dog would wait outside; I've seen this dog 'split a hedge' to turn the fox, and the two of them kept a free-range poultry farm clear of foxes for the nine years they worked together. Even as old dogs, they could do the job right to the edges, having worked the land together for so long that they knew where the foxes were going to run before the foxes themselves had decided.

The Catch

As with other quarry, different dogs have different ways of tackling their fox. The most usual way, and a favourite of Deerhound types, is to grip the fox across the back and ribcage (foxes are narrow beasts, and sighthound jaws are long) and deliver a mighty bite and shake. The bite not only crushes the spine and ribs, but destroys the internal organs, and the resulting damage is very similar to that caused by a well-placed rifle bullet. Once you take away the teeth, there isn't much to a fox, and such a death is extremely quick. Some dogs go for a neck hold, which is also very effective, and smaller dogs, especially Whippet types, can favour cruising alongside until a throat hold presents itself, being low enough to get in under the teeth and flip the fox over. My Deerhoundy J.B. would take hold across the spine immediately in front of the pelvis, the only dog I have ever seen do so, and break the spine there as well as by the terrific momentum of the shake, which had the heaviest part of the fox going over first, to smack into the ground either side of her. A dog needs to be strong in the neck to do this, though to look at this one, you would not have thought her capable, for though she was tall, she was very lightly built. Every bit as important is strength in the quarters, which have to support the dog as she lifts the fox. Some dogs don't really care where they grip the fox, and I have seen many pulled down by the brush, after which a spine hold is taken while nimbly dodging the sharp end.

In Cover

It is better all round if the first few foxes taken by the dog are coursed in the open, either by day or night. This is for two reasons: much of the fight is taken out of the fox if the dog runs it first – when you see the brush go up, you know you have a beaten fox – and the dog will be full of adrenaline and fired up for the tackle. Instinct is a great

The result of catching in a bramble thicket

thing, and instinct will cut in where experience may be lacking, and tell the dog what to do. However, foxes tend to lie up in cover, and if you don't have a flushing dog, a good many lurchers will be so keen that they will enter the cover and catch the fox within it. This means that the dog cannot shake the quarry, and there is little room for manoeuvre which favours the smaller, narrower fox. The dog may well get bitten in this case, and it is important for you to be on hand to minimise damage to either combatant – you may be killing foxes, but you don't want them to suffer, and nor your dog either. Most bites sustained by the dog in these circumstances are across the muzzle, whereas most bites from a fox tackled in the open tend to be to the upper foreleg. Get yourself into the cover and help your dog out as quickly as you can, then let her shake the dead fox as her reward. Terrier types, which are the most likely to enter cover, enjoy a prolonged rag at a fox carcase, whereas Deerhound and Saluki types usually lose interest once they have killed. If your dog has sustained a bite, do not continue to hunt with her, but take her home and deal with the injury at once, for a fox has a dirty bite and its teeth can go deeply.

First Aid

There are several ways of dealing with fox bites, which normally heal well and quickly on a healthy dog. Initially, you cannot beat salt-water bathing, and if there are deep punctures, swill these out by taking the water into a syringe. I add a few drops of Tea Tree oil to the first bathing, as this is a very strong, very safe antibacterial. Lavender oil makes a good alternative but is not quite as strong at Tea Tree. Only use salt water close to the eyes, for an accidental splash of that in the eyes will do no harm, but any antibacterial might. Some people then favour the use of a course of antibiotics. I don't use these, but I certainly wouldn't criticise anyone who does if that is their preference. Fox bites should be treated as soon as possible, and an extra first-aid kit carried in the vehicle is better than only having the one at home.

Muzzle wounds can swell alarmingly and be uncomfortable for the dog, and for these, there is a wonderful homoeopathic remedy called Mezerum*. Leg injuries are usually more straightforward unless the dog has been very unlucky and caught in the paw, and either will heal well given suitable attention. If you have two dogs, one will often lick the other's wounds, and should be allowed to, as this aids healing. Bite wounds should never be covered over, but left to the air to heal, and though they might look dramatic at first, they heal quickly and cleanly in a healthy animal. Always consult your vet if in doubt. Don't work a sore dog; wait until the bite is fully healed before you take her out again, even on rabbits, because it would be so easy for the dog to become a quitter if worked while she is still uncomfortable from the bite. If you have ever been bitten by a fox yourself, you will know exactly what I mean.

Support Training

Though no amount of training will make a fox dog where the will isn't there in the first place, being able to handle the dog onto a fox that you can see and the dog cannot can give success where a less well-trained dog would fail. One morning, I was walking the

*Mezerum 200C three times daily for ten days or as directed by a homoeopathic vet.

92

boundaries of a farm I used to hunt, when I saw a fox skulking along the edge of the woods. Being in cover myself, I could see better than the dogs, one of which was mine and had been trained to respond to quite complex signals. The other dog was quick on the uptake, and I hoped would take his cue from her. Gently restraining the second dog, I directed mine through the cover, over the brook and onto the fox's scent (never underestimate the scenting powers of even the most sighthoundy lurcher) and as she picked up the scent and dived into the wood, so I released the other dog, who went straight as an arrow across to join her. From my vantage point, I could see the fox, which the bitch boxed out of the wood and sent straight into the dog. A nice neat job which could never have been done if the bitch had not been trained to follow directions. The farmer was absolutely delighted.

The Bobbery Pack

A mixed pack which includes a lurcher or two can be a very efficient way of despatching foxes in wooded areas. Small noisy dogs with good noses are used to work through the woods and flush the foxes, and the lurcher is encouraged to wait on the outside of the cover, to course the fox once it is in the clear. With some blocks of cover, there are convenient viewpoints from which a handler can wait with their lurcher, though a dog is at a disadvantage if she starts her run down-hill, so these places need to be chosen with care. I have also known lurchers worked with a small mixed pack of crossbred hounds and terriers which hunted by scent like a pack of Foxhounds, except that once they went from drag to view, the lurcher took over to course the fox. In the latter case, they will often follow scent as easily as the scenting hounds, with the difference that lurchers have the tendency to look up as they get closer to their quarry (which they can tell both by changes in the scent and in the voice and demeanour of the pack) and once sighted, go like smoke. From the fox's point of view, there is little to tell it that it is in danger, because animals live in the present and do not speculate on a future that is outside their experience. A hunted fox that has escaped before has every confidence that it will escape again. By the time the lurcher is sighted and the fox is under pressure, it has only a few seconds in which to register that it is in trouble, and take evasive action. Either that works, in which case it reverts to going about its normal business, animals not being given to what-ifs, or it doesn't, in which case death is swift and humane, which is what we, as hunters, strive to achieve.

Lamping

Lamping with a lurcher is a good night-time method of fox catching in those areas where a rifle would be unsafe. Indeed, in many cases, the lurcher has the advantage over the firearm in that she never wounds, only tackles the correct target, and if something springs up in her way when she has been launched, she'll go round or even over it. I have seen my own dogs hurdle sheep on several occasions, and heard of one dog in hot pursuit of his fox who leaped over a roe deer. While a sensible lamper will make sure that he or she has the right quarry before launching the dog, anyone can make a mistake, and a properly trained dog will not get her owner into trouble by taking the wrong animal if the 'fox' suddenly turns into a small dog, the farm cat or even a stray lamb. Predators have binocular vision, that is, eyes at the front of the head, while herbivores have eyes at the sides of the head, to give better vision to the sides and behind. Thus, if you only see one eye, you are unlikely to be looking at a fox.

If foxes are lamped often, they become lamp-shy, and so will not come within range of the dog. In these cases, the rifle, assuming it is safe, is the weapon of choice, just as it may be more likely to do a better job if foxes are being lured in with bait, because foxes will come in at intervals if there is no fresh smell of dog to alert them. If, however, you are taking foxes by calling them in for the dog, you can be very successful assuming that the foxes have not been lamped before. The usual method is to go to a suitable area, and take a quick flash around with the lamp to see if you can pick up a pair of eyes shining green in the light. Many people like to use a coloured filter over the lamp for this first look around, in which case the colour of the eyes will not be the same as seen in a white light. Red filters are the most popular, though some people think blue is better as they have heard that animals do not see a blue light as well as a red or white one. Whether this is true or not is a moot point: whatever is used, the fox will learn from it, and not be fooled that way twice if the run is unsuccessful.

Having located your fox, you will seek to camouflage yourself by crouching down or backing into a tree trunk or other cover, and you need your dog to stay still and silent. Most lurchers catch on to this at once, and though you can feel them tremble beside you, they will neither move nor utter a sound. If yours does mutter anything, you are well-placed to give her a gentle elbow in the ribs (don't surprise her and make her yelp), but on no account speak – the fox will hear and be away at once. Whatever your views on the use of a slip, this is one time where it is essential at least in the early stages of training, for you do not want the dog to go until it is sent.

Once ready, start to call the fox in, and there are many ways of doing this. The simplest is to squeak your lips against your hand, but there are several different fox-calls that you can buy. Try them all and see what you prefer – I favour the little brass disc with a hole through the middle, but everyone has their favourite. For some reason, recorded calls are illegal in UK, which does seem rather odd. Some people are real artists at calling in a fox, the squeaks they produce being so lifelike and pathetic. Others can imitate different animals in distress, and foxes which are shy on a rabbit squeal can respond to a hare noise instead. At the right time of year, a cub call will bring an adult fox in, a different cub noise may call in other cubs, and in the breeding season the correct response to a vixen or dog-fox call can bring the appropriate animal within range, but not everyone can do these, and if you get them wrong, your fox will run away. Similarly, you are not likely to be successful if you make human noises or smells, for a cautious fox may well circle behind you to catch your scent on the wind. Calling in one fox and keeping it in sight, you may have another fox approaching from a different direction, and the first you will know of it will be your dog reacting. If there are two of you, it can be handy to split up, and for one person

A good catch on the lamp

95

to call the fox so that it comes in across the line of sight of the person with the dog, which is something else that you could not risk with a rifle. Arrange beforehand how you are going to lamp: most people favour a very quick flash around after a few calls, but I have known successful lampers who believed in keeping the lamp on throughout the calling process.

Foxes are amazing at using the contours of the land to assist their escape, and you should not allow yourself to be disappointed with your dog when she doesn't connect with every fox she runs. Sometimes you can have them there in the lamp, and they just seem to vapourise and disappear into the darkness. As a dog learns her trade, she will become adept at working her fox away from cover, boxing it back out into the open, and all the time be ready to put in a decisive strike. This is where a made rabbit dog will have the advantage, for she will already be well-versed in dominating her quarry rather than simply following it.

Once the fox has come into a good position, and close enough that the dog can put real pressure on it, slip the dog and keep the beam on the fox. When the dog connects, keep the lamp on, and run towards the dog, which will further faze the fox if it is still alive, and give your dog support. This is especially important with early training, as foxes are slippery customers, and if the dog does miss her grip or collect a bite, the fox could still get away. Even a made dog can slip at the critical time, and no fox is a certainty until you have the body in your hands. You cannot tell how easy or difficult any fox will be until you run it, so be there to help your dog if need be. It is all too easy to get complacent when you have a good foxer, and take for granted that the dog will succeed every time without any help at all. I was guilty of this once, when the dog caught his fox on the lip of a hollow, and I wasn't across the field in time to help when he lost his balance and the fox pulled away from him. This had never happened before and nor did it afterwards, for I try to learn from my mistakes. The big yellow vixen, which had been taking lambs, managed to eel through the bottom of a stock-fence over which, being against a blackthorn hedge, the dog could not follow. It seemed unbelievable that a fox could get through such a tiny gap, but she could and did, and by the time we had found a place to get over, there was no sign of her. I knew she was mortally injured by the amount of blood, and eventually we found her body, but it was not as good a job done as I would have wished. She was a very expensive vixen, too, for my dog had broken a toe, which was probably what had caused him to lose his hold in the first place, and he was off work for months with complications arising from this injury.

For the most part, a fox will either come in straight away, sometimes at a run, or not at all. Don't squeak constantly, or at the same strength, but pause often, vary your call, and make it very weak at times, as if the stricken rabbit were almost finished. If your fox hasn't responded after a few minutes of calling, it isn't going to. Some come in very cautiously, run and stop, run and stop, but a few, especially that year's youngsters in the early autumn when the crops have just come off, will come in really fast and almost right up to you. If you live in the kind of area in which urban-captured foxes are turned out, or else 'rescued' foxes which have been taken in by animal sanctuaries are subsequently released, you will get spates of finding foxes which are neither wary of dogs nor able to hunt for themselves, and these usually come in fast, and can be upon you really quickly, especially the very hungry ones. Killing these foxes is an act of mercy: they don't cope in the wild and are the most likely to predate on domestic stock. Some carry considerable injuries and surgical scars; my Bedlington lurcher once picked up a vixen so light that she must have been starving, and she had a long scar from stifle to the point of one hip, very obviously veterinary in origin. She was also in breeding fettle, perhaps had even been mated. The outcome of her bearing a litter would have included a great deal of suffering, for it was clear that she barely had the ability to feed herself.

Other foxes we have caught include a high proportion with three legs, the stump on the fourth often seeming to have had veterinary intervention. Of course, it is perfectly possible for foxes to lose a leg in, say, a traffic accident, and make a good recovery if there is sufficient food, without any human help, so perhaps we simply have a lot of clumsy foxes about. Dumped foxes in the area I live in now tend to be unusually fat, with nice shiny coats, whereas a few years ago we would get periodic influxes of fat but mange-ridden foxes. I assume that the diseased ones come straight from urban back gardens, where the scavenging is good but the food quality is poor, while those in good condition have had a spell of medical treatment at some animal sanctuary. Certainly, you don't get overweight wild foxes, and though you will find wild foxes with broken or worn-down teeth, you don't find them with a thick layer of tartar typical of a diet of junk food or else the cheaper sorts of commercial pet food. The Union of Country Sports Workers is currently conducting a countrywide survey of such animals, and the results will be very interesting.

Digging

A lurcher can be an asset where foxes are being dug out of their earths. The process is not dissimilar to ferreting, but on a larger scale. The holes that serve the earth are either netted or blocked, and the terrier, which wears a locator collar, allowed to enter. Once the terrier has found the fox, she will seek to bolt it, or else hold it at bay. If the former, the fox will either bolt into a net, from where it will be humanely despatched, or it will sneak out of an uncovered exit if one has been missed. In the latter case, the lurcher's superior senses should alert her to the fox's imminent departure, and she will often be in the right place to catch the fox as it exits, or else pursue it as it runs away. Sometimes even the lurcher will miss the fox's depart-ure, but the corvids won't, and a sudden chattering of magpies or screech of a jay ought to be heeded. A fleeing fox is by no means

After the dig

easy to catch in these circumstances, especially if the terrain is difficult or well-covered in undergrowth, but many lurchers excel at this type of fox control.

If the fox is held at bay by the terrier, then it must be dug down to, and in the process, another fox may bolt. Equally, if a litter of young cubs is being dug out, the vixen may bolt unexpectedly. Sentimental souls might think that she would stay to defend her cubs, but Nature doesn't work like that, and an adult fox almost always chooses to bolt and save itself, sometimes returning for the cubs later when it thinks the coast is clear. While fox hunts have a voluntary close season while foxes are breeding, pest controllers do not, and so despatch of many litters occurs each year in those areas where no foxes are tolerated.

If there is only one fox and it does not bolt, there comes a stage where the person digging breaks through to the terrier and fox facing each other, lifts out the terrier and despatches the fox. Fox hunts and pest controllers use a humane killer or suitable pistol for this work, for which appropriate paperwork has to be held.

Starting

I prefer to start a dog foxing on the lamp for several reasons. The dog is used to following the beam, and so has no doubt that the fox is legitimate quarry. The fox can be called in closely, and so the handler can control when the dog is released, and on which quarry she runs (if a rabbit gets up as a daytime fox comes by, a novice dog may hesitate momentarily, which is enough to lose either quarry). The fox will have had a hard run for fifty to a hundred yards before it is tackled, which gives greater advantage to the dog, both because the fox is running out of steam, and the dog's blood is up. Foxes are much more active at night, and further from home, so there is more chance of finding what you want with sufficient room to operate to the dog's advantage. The whole event is much more tightly controlled by the handler: there will be time enough in the future for the dog to use her initiative. With a bitch, try to start her at the time following her season where she would have had pups, as a lot of bitches can be very assertive then. However, the saying about best-laid plans is as true here as anywhere; some dogs will self-enter at any time, and some foxes will present themselves for catching during the day or when the dog might not be ready. A brace of pups that I bred caught their first fox together at seven months old, and their jaws were barely strong enough to kill it, but another pup from the same litter went into his first fox at ten months, got bitten, and never faced another. The bitch that I kept was not used on fox until she was three – late entering even for me – and became a heller on fox. I only kept her back because I could not find the 'right' fox for her to start on – the right fox being one with plenty of space around it for her to course and catch in the open. One of my gamekeeper friends, a first-rate dogman, commented that he had never known a dog ruined by entering it too late. Her son, in contrast, self-entered before his second birthday by pulling a fox out of a hedge while we were out walking, and retrieving it alive, a spitting, hissing bundle like a giant red moustache. He then pinned it at my feet, and his aged grandmother (who had been a fine foxer in her day) doddered up, sized up the situation, leaned forward to bite expertly and neatly through its neck and wandered off again. Job done, and he, too, became a committed and enthusiastic foxer.

Opportunism

You are likely to catch as many foxes on an opportunist basis as you will from careful planning. Simply going for a walk with a made fox dog will find foxes if they are there to be found, especially if your dog has a good nose. I had to stop taking one of my dogs foot-following the local hunt as he was so good at marking foxes in cover, and became so frustrated when he wasn't allowed to follow up his finds. Other times, we have found foxes in broad daylight right beside well-used public rights of way. Of course, a walk through town early in the morning will find many foxes going about their business, tidying up takeaway leftovers, tearing open rubbish bags, or slipping over garden walls to check for food in the form of hutched pets. On a bitter day, rural foxes will be tucked up in dense cover, to the lee of the wind, or in a cosy hollow, and if it is sunny, they often will lie out in the warm. Close to human habitat, they like woodpiles, silage bales and barns full of hay or straw, and can take quite a bit of evicting from there, for many of these places are unsafe to put a dog in. Sometimes a larger dog will manage where a terrier-size risks falling down a gap between bales and getting stuck, and a pack of hounds going into these kind of places can give spectacular results. Foxes are creatures of habit, which is often their undoing. If they find free-range poultry or new lambs, and a good place to lie up close by, they will wait on and find out the farmer's schedule over several days. It is not uncommon to spring a fox that has been waiting for the poultry to be let out in the mornings. I remember grading eggs one morning, when the farm dog bounded into a nearby ditch and bolted a fox, which took refuge in the woodpile at

Among the straw bales

such speed that it was clear she had done so before. While he held the fox at bay at the front of the woodpile, my fawn bitch slunk round the back, and as soon as the fox started to reverse out, she grabbed her by the brush and started to draw her. Once the hindquarters were in sight, she changed her grip so fast that the eye could not register, and caught the vixen in her preferred grip just forward of the pelvis, crunching through spine and soft tissue. By the time she had extracted the sharp end, there was little life left in the vixen, and another poultry killer had been brought to book.

Misunderstandings

Don't be in too much of a hurry to think that your dog will be no good as a foxer if early encounters don't go entirely to plan. I make no apology for going back to the very young dog – before a potential foxer is ready, she might indeed be shy of closing with this particular quarry, yet what a difference maturity can make. A dog that takes care of itself will be an asset where a hot-head that steams in without thinking is not necessarily the best type. Many young

Mixed bag

lurchers will show no interest in a dead fox, even one that they have seen caught by another dog, and certainly few are interested in a cold carcase that you may show them to encourage them. If you have run a dog over two years old several times with a proven dog, and she has made no attempt to connect with the fox, it is not time to write her off until you have run her solo. It could be her deference to the other dog which is keeping her back But if, even run solo with everything in her favour, she does not catch when she has had a good chance of doing so, she probably does not have it in her to do that job. A dog which is really trying may well not connect, because foxes aren't easy, but she should be making that fox twist and turn. If that is the case, then she simply needs more practice. If the fox is not doing much to evade her, then she isn't putting pressure on it, and if she gives mouth, then she is afraid. This does not mean that she is a useless lurcher – there are excellent dogs which will not take fox – but it does mean that this is not her job, and there is nothing you can do to change that.

4 The Hare-Coursing Lurcher

Competitive and Pot-Filling

The relationship between the lurcher and the hare is unique, for among the lurcher's traditional quarry, only the hare has such sporting credentials. Though the lurcher's primary job as pot-filler meant catching hares for food – and it used to be said that one hare would feed a poor family for a week – the lurcher has a different role for pest control, due to the hare's irregular distribution in the UK. Hares are extremely plentiful in some areas, where their impact on crops, forestry and grazing is significant (we must never forget that grass is a crop, and just as valuable as corn) but there are also areas of the UK where hares are so scarce that a sight of one is a welcome treat. The hare is not, as some would believe, rare, for the hare population is just over twice that of the fox, which nobody could describe as rare (approximately 500,000 foxes to approximately one million brown hares, allowing for seasonal variations. Pre-hunting-ban figures provided by scientific research from The Game Conservancy: fox and hare populations are expected to alter significantly now that the excellent wildlife management provided by hunting and legal coursing has been suspended). But it is scarce in certain areas, and so its culling by any means cannot be justified in such places. Hares and rabbits do not co-exist well, and areas low in hares tend to have large rabbit populations, whereas areas with plenty of hares have correspondingly fewer rabbits. Therefore truly ethical lurcher owners who course the hare as a sporting animal and for pest control travel to hare-rich places to do so if hares are scarce in their own area.

The Blue Hare

Native to Britain is the blue hare, *Lepus timidus*, also known as the snow or mountain hare, which was often kept as a pet in early times when its range covered the whole of the British Isles. (It is from the role as pet that 'puss' became a popular reference to a hare, apparently before the same name was used for cats. We still refer to hares as 'puss' or 'sally'). The term 'blue' refers to the winter pelage

Blue hare country

Kelpie lurcher with
rabbits and blue hare
(*D. Sleight*)

of this handsome hare, which changes from brown to white as the weather worsens. The modern Irish hare is so close genetically to the blue hare that they are almost certainly from the same stock. Nowadays, the blue hare's range is restricted to the higher parts of northern England and Scotland. As a quarry, it is considered similar to the rabbit in that it is testing, but not in the same league as the brown hare, of which more shortly. Inhabiting rough, hilly country, the blue hare is a master of using gradient, long heather, rocks and holes in the ground to evade a pursuing dog, and it takes a tough dog to catch this hare on its preferred terrain on a regular basis. Once on less testing ground, however, the blue hare is fairly easily caught by an averagely competent dog. Thus this hare is hunted nowadays for pest control and animal food (it is considered inferior eating to the brown hare) though in hungrier times it made a perfectly acceptable addition to the poor man's table.

The Brown Hare

The brown hare, *Lepus europaeus* or *Lepus capensis*, is different altogether in sporting terms. It was probably brought to Britain by the Romans, who liked their coursing, as both a food and a sporting animal, and has served this dual purpose ever since. Brown hares are larger than blue, averaging about seven pounds in weight, and can cause appreciable agricultural damage where they exist in high numbers. Hares are taken by lurchers in several ways, from the gate-net, now not used so often as in the old days when it was probably the most favoured method involving a dog, to being picked up out of its seat in a typically opportunist lurcher manner, and of course what is regarded by many as the cream of field sports, by coursing. The gate-net has been described in the chapter on rabbiting, so let us look at the other methods.

Out of the Seat

Hares live above ground, though they will seek refuge underground if pressed, in a rabbit burrow or a drainage pipe, for instance. Normally, they lie in shallow scrapes called 'forms' where they can see predators while considering themselves concealed. The hare is beautifully camouflaged and very difficult to see when resting in this fashion. Hares have almost 360 degree vision, with only a small blind spot to the front and rear, at the nose and the back of the head. The mooching lurcher is capable of following the hare's scent almost to its form, but hares don't allow their scent trail to lead right up to their resting-place, instead using a series of prodigious leaps to foil the scent-hunting predator. It is marvellous to watch the lurcher, which has followed the scent eagerly until this point, casting herself hither and yon, trying to find a thread of scent which will lead her to her quarry. So long as the hare stays still she (hares are always known as 'she') will give off almost no scent, and I say 'almost' advisedly because I have seen enough lurchers find enough hares to know that, while there is hardly any scent, there will be a minute amount. A lurcher can change from sight to scent hound in a second, and indeed it is my experience that even pure-bred sighthounds are perfectly capable of using their noses well enough to find a hidden hare. For us humans, it is sight alone that finds the hare; spotting a hare in a field is a knack that takes a fair bit of experience to develop. It is said that if you see a clod of earth in a field and it gets smaller as you walk towards it, it is a hare, but if it gets bigger, it is a clod of earth. I can't begin to tell you of the number of clods of earth I have seen get up and run.

Meanwhile, the lurcher is testing what little scent she can find, tacking from side to side, and is closing in on her hare. Some have refined the skill of taking the hare straight out of her seat, which is the pot-filler's way as it takes little out of the dog. Foxes are very good at catching hares this way as well. But once the hare lifts and starts to run, it takes speed and commitment to catch her, as well as that indefinable something known as 'quarry sense' which is anticipation of how and where the hare will run.

Running

It takes a good dog to catch daytime hares regularly. The brown hare has been described as the supreme mammalian athlete: it is fast, tremendously agile, and has terrific endurance. Almost a third of its body is taken up by the hindlegs and their musculature, and its heart and lungs are vast for its size. Sprinting hounds such as Greyhounds – the fastest dogs in the world – have around one minute to catch their hare before they run out of speed, but purpose-bred lurchers are capable of coursing for as long as six minutes, and longer courses – known as 'gruellers' – are well-known. Even then, the hare frequently gets away, and if it does, the hunter tips his hat to it and wishes it well, for as Arrian wrote long ago, 'The true hunter does not set out to catch the hare, but delights in the challenge of the course, and is pleased when the hare escapes.' Arrian also mentions occasions when he has released a hare that one of his

Athletes all: compare the size of dog and hare

dogs has caught after an exceptional course, showing not only that he was a consummate sportsman, but also that he had soft-mouthed hounds.

In common with all prey species, the hare only runs as fast as it needs, and so will run more slowly ahead of a slow dog than it will with a fast one. Indeed, hares have often been seen to be apparently toying with a dog that is too slow to pose a threat to them, twisting and turning them all over the landscape until, tiring of the game, the hare finds another gear and accelerates away with contemptuous ease. Thus slower lurchers must develop other skills to pick up their hare – and they do. Some learn to read the hare so that they sidestep and catch it as it feints one way and then turns the other, some, especially the endurance-bred dogs, persistently box the hare away from refuge until it makes a mistake, others wait behind it at half-speed, giving the hare the impression that it has the measure of them, then accelerate in a short, blinding burst to pick up. But a good hare is equal to any of it, which is what makes them such a respected quarry. Coursing is a very selective way of catching hares in that usually only the sick, old or otherwise lesser animals are taken. Indeed, post-mortem evidence on coursed hares submitted to the Burns Enquiry showed that, while most of the hares examined seemed by their appearance to be in good health, all of them were in fact ailing in some way.

Competitive Coursing

Competitive lurcher coursing is based on the same set of National Coursing Club (NCC) rules that serve Greyhound coursing, and that of other sighthounds in UK, there being clubs for Salukis, Whippets and Scottish Deerhounds. Only in lurcher coursing, however, do you get the division between single-handed i.e. one dog one hare, and doubled-up, which is the more conventional scene of two dogs on one hare. For many, including myself, the purest of coursing is between a single dog and a hare, and there are few sights to touch the contest between the dog and the hare running across the landscape, of which the hare knows every inch and every refuge, and the dog knows only how to read the hare and try to match its evasive techniques.

Central to competitive coursing is the concept of 'fair law', which is the distance a hare is allowed to travel before the dogs are released. This distance differs with the different types of hound that are coursed, Greyhounds having longer distances before they are slipped (typically 80 to 100 yards) than Whippets (60 plus yards). Competitive coursing lurchers, having speed, height and endurance, give the hare the longest 'law' of all, 100 yards minimum, and I have seen dogs held back by the slipper (the official in charge of releasing them) for a full two hundred yards before being sent, which results in a tremendous run-up i.e. the full-pelt gallop to get up to the hare. The coursed hare often lets the dogs get right up to it before it starts its incredible evasive tactics, and it is an amazing sight as dogs and hare conduct a duel at around thirty miles plus per hour. Though many dogs can get up to their hare quickly, it is in working it that they show their talents best, and this is pure

Hare

instinct, for you cannot train it in. Strike was covered in the rabbit chapter: strangely, strike is often absent in otherwise excellent coursing lurchers. I suspect this is because these dogs are fielded so fit, and have so much endurance that they are not pressed by the need to bring the course to an end. They can afford to wait, and they know it. Lacking understanding of the competitive aspect that some human owners find so important, the dog does not seek to save its energy for future courses that day, but locks on to its hare, seeing and hearing nothing else until either the hare is caught or lost. This means that the dog with strike can end a lot of courses quickly and to its advantage, whereas dogs that lack it can take too much out of themselves each time they course. Lurchers are coursed a lot more frequently than Greyhounds because of the scoring: there are no points for a kill under NCC rules, but in doubled-up competitive lurcher coursing, though other aspects of NCC scoring are usually upheld, the catch sometimes earns extra points depending on how the course has been run. With single-handed coursing competitions, it is only the catch that earns points.

Breeding

Lurchers used in competitive coursing are almost always a mixture of Saluki and Greyhound, though there are famous strains of coursers which have other breeds, such as Deerhound, in the

Saluki Greyhound

ancestry. The idea is to have the endurance of the Saluki wedded to the speed of the Greyhound, and purpose-bred coursing lurchers certainly have plenty of both. These are then crossed with other Saluki/Greyhound composites, and the coursing field determines the most talented dogs from which to breed. Running the brown hare week in, week out during the season is the most ruthless selection process.

Bloodlines are carefully kept, and pups bred from match coursing dogs change hands for a lot of money.

Conditioning

A book could be written on this subject alone. The coursing lurcher is usually treated to the best of food and medical care, and fitness programmes are closely-guarded secrets. It takes real stockmanship to keep these dogs so fit and still have enough leeway to bring them up to match fitness, letting them down afterwards but not too much because they will be run again so soon. It would be difficult to envisage any dog in any discipline that is fielded fitter than a match coursing hound: they are all muscle, bone and sinew with not a trace of fat or superfluous flesh. Their coats glow with health, and they move like the athletes they are. Greed will always get the better of some people, though, and there are a very few who use drugs in this game, just as the same substances crop up in horse and Greyhound training, not to mention that of human athletes. Not only does this tarnish the whole sport, it ruins the health of the animal to which it has been given, and is a deplorable business. I would not want to leave the subject of match coursing with this nasty taste, so reflect that far more successful dogs are kept to the very best of the owner's ability, honestly coursed, and want for nothing.

The Fens

Fenland coursing is legendary, and while the hare is never an easy quarry, and different areas provide different challenges to the hare-catching lurcher, the big-sky country of the Fens produces some of the most spectacular coursing in the UK. Because the Fens are flat and open, the coursing dogs used there have enormous stamina. Nor is the coursing slow, for Fenland hares, like West Country stags, are nourished on good crops, are larger than in other parts of the country, and really can run. While I have seen hares coursed well all over the UK, there is a special magic on the Fens. It is not often that a place or an event surpasses its publicity, but this is something utterly splendid. My grateful thanks to the people who invited and looked after me on those unforgettable sporting days.

Fenland coursing dogs – crème de la crème

Waiting out of sight of the coursed hare

Lurcher Clubs

Lurcher clubs are very protective of the land they course over and the landowners who allow them to do so, for without them this marvellous sport could not exist. As well as paying a fee to the landowner, legitimate lurcher clubs undertake to protect the hares from poachers and foxes, their two main enemies, and often help the landowner in other ways as well, such as with farm work at busy times, or on the shoot, as many farms run a small shoot, and with year-round pest control. Entry to these associations is necessarily difficult, and a thorough vetting of applicants takes place. Often, people are only accepted after a season on 'trial' during which they have to bring some positive benefit to the club.

Poachers

'Poachers' referred to in hare terms are not the one-for-the-pot types that most landowners will tolerate so long as they do no damage and don't call too frequently, but bands of marauding thugs who are sometimes erroneously called 'illegal coursers'. These people have no respect for land, hare or landowner, driving across fields, wrecking crops, gates, fences and hedges, running packs of dogs on hares and harassing the hares even in the breeding season. They have a reputation for stealing dogs, and for abandoning them when they have served their turn or become injured. They frequently return to the land for other criminal activities, and are a bane to genuine lurcher men and women, who are often tarred with the same brush by those who have a grudge against all lurcherwork. Genuine lurcher coursers treat their dogs (which are often also family pets) like royalty, give them every care while working and a decent retirement at the end. They observe a strict close season so that the hares may breed in peace, unless the landowner has an unusually high population in which case sensible local culling will be carried out. Being true countrymen and women, they act as extra eyes and ears to the landowner, and can be very useful in all sorts of ways, just like the lurcher itself.

Moving Hares

In areas where there is a large hare population, hare shoots are held, which cull enormous numbers of hares and of course are non-selective. Hares can absorb a lot of lead before they die, and many shooting people refuse to shoot hares with shotguns because of this. Hare shoots generally take place right at the end of the season, to allow the coursing clubs and the beaglers their chance to weed out the weaker specimens, and some estates then allow hare drives before the shoots. (Following the 2005 Waterloo Cup, 3,500 hares were shot on the same land in two days. This was because there would be no coursing thereafter until the 2005 Hunting ban was repealed.) Coursing clubs help out in two ways. One is by organising hare drives where the hares are driven into long-nets, then captured unhurt and put into special travelling boxes. The hares are then transported to estates where they are welcome, to refresh the gene pool of the local stock or perhaps to re-introduce hares where they were once present but have disappeared for one reason or another. Hares are incredibly sensitive to agriculture, and modern farming methods do not suit them because they need a steady supply of food and shelter all year round. Farmers who have taken on new ground and reverted to a more hare-friendly type of farming, and would like to have a few around, obtain them in this way. If the numbers thrive and grow to the point where they have to be controlled, this is easily done, and such farmers are the true backbone of wildlife management. Another reason for hare populations rising, falling and even failing completely, is their own health, for overcrowding brings with it not only various diseases but stress, and hares cope badly with stress. Where the poaching gangs harass them, they do not have to kill all the hares to empty an area of them, because the stress either kills the hares or drives them away. Regarding disease, there are several that will take a hare population beyond sustainability, such as hare syphilis, coccidiosis and grass sickness. Unlike rabbits, hares do not seem to catch myxomatosis. The other great hare killer, the fox, can never be underestimated, for one pair of foxes can empty an area of hares simply by killing that year's population of leverets, which were the following year's breeding stock. Once the fox population has been culled, hares can be re-introduced and will probably thrive as long as the fox control continues.

The transported hares have six to nine months to learn their new territory, and so by the time that coursing starts again, they are as confident as the hares that were bred there, and every bit as difficult to catch.

The other way that lurchers can help is by 'sweeping' after the shoots, thereby picking up the wounded for humane despatch. This should not be taken as any criticism of the shooting, for the hare is not an easy animal to kill instantly with a shotgun, and sadly, injured hares are inevitable after hare shoots. No other method is as efficient as that of a trained dog, which will find, catch and retrieve hare after hare. Wounded hares are still capable of running hard, such is their amazing physique, and only coursing dogs can be relied upon to catch them quickly. There is benefit for the dogs, too, for easy catches improve a young or inexperienced dog's confidence no end, while for the old dog well past her best, there is fulfilment in still being able to succeed in her work.

Lamping

This is a very controversial subject amongst lurcher owners, for the lamped hare is nothing like as difficult to catch as the daytime hare. To many, the hare is such a special animal that to catch it any other way than by coursing is an insult. Certainly, dogs that could never catch a daytime hare given fair law are able to catch them by night. However, realistically, if hares are a pest in a particular area, and the only dog you have available cannot catch them by day, then the hares have to be lamped. Not everyone keeps a coursing dog, or wants to, and lamping the hare is just a different way of catching them, in the same way that gate-netting, taking them out of the seat,

Sometimes hares must be lamped (*Phil Lloyd*)

or shooting is. However, if you want to be proud of having a hare-catching dog, it is better not to boast of catches in the lamp.

One for the Pot

Much as I enjoy seeing the line of beaters string out across the land to walk-up the hares while one or a brace of dogs strain at their slips, much as I admire the sagacity which leads a dog to a hare that is sitting in her form, to lift and retrieve her before she realises, for me there is nothing quite like walking the land with a single lurcher, watching the dog hunting-up using her nose and then changing to sighthound as the hare lifts ahead of us. Small fields, large fields, open land, hills or plains, all ask different questions of a dog, and rare is the dog that can bring a hare on terms in every area. Being a specialist on her own ground is no disgrace, and I love to watch dog and hare stretched out against the landscape, in a tableau as old as Time.

A tableau as old as Time *(Roly Boughton)*

Hares in Europe

There are relatively few places in Europe where *Lepus europaeus* is coursed the way it is in the UK. Southern Ireland has its Park Coursing, but that is a world away from lurcher work, being for Greyhounds only, and a completely different activity from Greyhound coursing in England. Park coursing involves hares being brought into the area and kept contained in the wild but inside a fence. They are allowed time to accustom themselves to their new home, and are driven up the Park course every day so that they know the escape routes, which are gaps under the end of the track which will let a hare through but not a dog. When the day of the competition arrives, the hares are driven through one by one, and as they have learned, they run straight up the prepared route and out of one of the escape routes at the end, from whence they then go free. The Greyhounds, usually muzzled, run straight up after them, sometimes without putting in any turns, and so the competition is judged largely on speed. Irish coursing Greyhounds are huge dogs, and weights in excess of ninety pounds running fit are not uncommon. Because the Irish hare does not offer such speed as the brown hare, brown hares used to be imported for coursing from time to time, and a friend of mine recollects an incident where the hares, released into the fenced Park, pinged over the fence and just kept going. Obviously someone neglected to explain to them what they were supposed to do.

Formal coursing is illegal in some European countries, though informal coursing is another matter, and may be conducted discreetly if not entirely lawfully. Iberian countries have an assortment of attractive sighthounds, such as the Galgo and the Maltese hound, which are used perfectly legally for hunting in a similar manner to the lurcher.

Skills

Coursing lurchers often retrieve their hares, rather cocking a snook at those who say that Saluki lurchers do not retrieve. I have personally seen retrieves on the Fens of well over a mile. Fen-coursing dogs are not all that big, and Fenland hares are, ten pounders being regularly caught, so that is quite a feat. I remember standing by a cover crop watching a course that had lasted easily five minutes, when the hare leapt the dyke beside me and went into the cover. Most Greyhounds would have pulled up, but not a lurcher; the dog went straight in and after a burst of crackling through the rough there was that familiar gruff nasal squeal as the dog picked up his hare. He came out of the cover, sighted his owner half a mile away, looked at me, slung the hare (now deceased) at my feet with a look of 'Here, take this, will you? These things are damned heavy, you know' leapt the dyke and ran back to his owner, leaving me to carry a nice hare which was indeed damned heavy.

Dangers

Anyone coursing hares is advised to familiarise the dog with the lie of the land before she ever runs behind a hare. Hares are adept at writing off their pursuers, and will deliberately lead a dog into farm machinery, or take refuge under buildings or dumped rubbish. The dog, with eyes for nothing but her quarry, can be injured or even killed this way. Country with big drainage ditches, such as Fen dykes, Somerset rhines or rheens, or Sussex rifes, can cause awful damage unless the dog has been taught how to leap them. A dog that meets one of these obstacles the wrong way commonly hits the far side at full speed instead of clearing the full width, which often results in one or both front legs breaking, or else the spine if the dog falls backwards into the dyke. Then there is the risk of drowning if nobody is close by to assist (a horse nearly drowned in a Sussex rife near me only a short time ago – that is how deep they are). Other parts of the country, with steep hillsides, rocky outcrops, gravel slopes or deep clay mud will also ask a great deal of a coursing lurcher. Hares are often found where the land carries a lot of flint, and flint that meets farm machinery gets sliced into pieces sharper than most knives. Barbed wire will tear a dog, but flint will cripple her, cutting through tendons to cause irreparable damage. I know of a coursing Greyhound bitch running her last course before being retired as her owner's pet, which trod on a single flint while coursing on good going in Hampshire. She cut through tendons, vein and artery on one leg, and despite swift veterinary attention, could not be saved in a condition that would have allowed her quality of life. The heartbroken owner won the cup and lost his favourite dog.

Competitive coursing dogs peak early, retire early, and then have probably half of their lives left in which to do other lurcher jobs, so it makes good sense for them to be trained just like any other lurcher when they are pups. A season on rabbits will certainly improve their

One for the pot . . . and another approaching

119

strike, and encourage them to get up to their quarry without delay, which in turn will take less out of them than the dog which only sees hares and so runs longer courses. A desire to get the job done is beneficial to owner and dog alike, and even when there are no trophies to be won, a dog that has the skill and experience to end a course as quickly as possible, will fill the freezer. I love to watch a long course over open country; it is pure venery, but I am bound to admit that the hound which catches her hare in the same field that she sprang it from is probably the better lurcher.

5 The King's Deer

History of the Venison Provider

The deer is a most natural quarry for a dog, and any breed of dog will show a ready interest in them. In canine terms, there is a far better meat-to-effort ratio in catching a deer than in catching a rabbit, and deer is one of the few quarry species to which a dog needs no formal entering – they are born wanting to hunt them. Indeed, I know of more than one dog that caught her first deer before her first rabbit. Mankind has hunted deer since the dawn of time, initially for food, and then, as we became settled farmers, for pest control as well. Nowadays, the pest control is every bit as important as the venison, for deer cause significant damage to crops, hedges, fences and forestry. In our overcrowded island, deer populations need to be managed for the sake of the deer themselves as well as the habitat they share with other wild creatures. Little has changed between the deer and the dog since we first domesticated the wolf: laws and kings come and go, but the relationship between the dog and the deer endures.

Background

Until William the Conqueror brought his Norman ways to Britain, the natives had enjoyed total freedom to hunt. Indeed, hunting is burned into the psyche of the British. These islands were famed for their huge hounds, used in war and for the hunt, but in this book, we are only concerned with the latter. Because of the dense forestry that covered much of the land, deer were often hunted by a series of hounds: lymers found them, running mastiffs and scent-hounds pursued them, but it took two very different types of hound to bring them to book: fast-running dogs which hunted by sight alone – mentioned by Arrian and being called Vertragi, or else with holding mastiffs which would either hold the deer at bay or pull them down and hold them until the huntsmen arrived. When animals are hunted for food, a torn carcase is undesirable, and so hunting dogs were bred to hold the quarry until the hunters could kill it. Regardless of fanciful paintings etc., this is how the majority of quarry was despatched, and the same method is used today in New Zealand and Australia where feral pigs formidable in size are hunted in dense forestry with teams of dogs – dogs to find, to 'bail' i.e. hold at bay, and to hold without damaging until the hunters can catch up and administer the *coup de grâce*.

Queen Elizabeth I would shoot driven deer with a crossbow, and one of her huntsmen once leapt from his horse onto the hunted stag's back, and killed it at her feet, using his sword, which apparently pleased her very much. Modern staghunts in the UK pride themselves on their hounds never touching their quarry, but instead holding it at bay until shot at point-blank range by a member of the Hunt staff.

Use of a sight-hunting dog is, however, different. The dog needs to be able to kill the deer fast and cleanly: though some show an inclination to hold a deer and wait for assistance, the best dogs for deer work have an inborn knack of despatching their quarry astonishingly quickly. Especially in the old poaching days, any sounds of struggle would draw unwanted attention, so a dog that could course and kill swiftly was a 'must'. There is also the humanity issue: virtually any dog of terrier size and above can catch one of our smaller deer, but what is needed is a dog that can effect a neat kill in as short a time as possible.

Locally to me there used to live a brace of Border terriers that wrought havoc among the roe until they 'disappeared' one day, and it is quite common for pet dogs (in particular a pair of Golden Retrievers I knew of, that were allowed to run riot) to cause unforgivable injuries. Certain organisations with an axe to grind have been known to display posters showing grievously damaged deer, the captions stating that these injuries were caused by lurchers. In truth, such damage is more often caused by out-of-control pets, for the working lurcher is a professional. Exceptions do occur, however. There is no doubt that idiots are in plentiful supply in all walks of life, and there have been incidents of poachers tarnishing the true image of lurchers and lurcherwork by driving vehicles over land and through fences, unleashing packs of dogs on deer, and carnage to both dogs and deer being the result. There is nothing to be proud of in a dog being dragged by a deer through hedges and trees, nor in several dogs being used to bring down a small deer that could have been neatly grassed and despatched by a single dog that knows its trade. These people are no more hunters than football hooligans are athletes, but they have done untold damage to the image of the lurcher, especially with regard to deer work. Then you have people who prefer a good tale to the tedious truth: I was recently stopped by a farmhand who, looking pointedly at my dogs, told me that poachers had left a dead deer in the fields. Why would a poacher leave all that meat behind? When I went to check, the carcase was that of a fox.

We still have tracts of thick woodland in parts of the country, and if a fast-running dog is used after deer in this sort of area, it is virtually certain that the dog will be injured, probably badly or even terminally, before long. Therefore the sensible hunter waits to take deer out in the open, which is easier with some species of deer than others. Once sprung, the deer has little distance to make before being overtaken and dropped by a good running dog, which is useful on small farms, the deer usually being taken in one field. This avoids complications with neighbouring landowners. I do remember early one Sunday morning getting an urgent telephone call from a farmer whose dog had caught a roe deer just across the boundary of a not terribly sporting neighbour. I was a twenty-minute drive away, and en route found a roe buck that had just been hit by a car, so into the back of the van it went. Arriving at the farm, I picked up the farmer and we drove across the fields to the boundary, where we left the vehicle, then we climbed over a ditch and through two barbed wire fences to where her dog was lying beside the deer. In typical lurcher fashion, he had tripped it and dropped it without fuss or unnecessary damage, and now was guarding it until we could help. When he saw us, he assumed the biggest grin and there was much tail-wagging and bouncing: he was only a sapling and this was his first roe. I must say, I did feel rather conspicuous as the farmer and I, two very respectable middle-aged ladies, struggled this big buck back across the field and ditch and under the two fences, at seven o'clock on a Sunday morning. Into the van it went with the other one, and off we drove to the farmhouse and a celebratory breakfast, with a very happy lurcher joining in.

Natural Selection

Given the option, a dog will always seek to take the weakest deer, and many deer that are brought to book by a lurcher will be found to have something wrong with them. Using a dog is also the best way to find a wounded deer that is lying-up, though great care should be taken not to be injured by it. During my deer-catching days, I found some amazing injuries. There was the very underweight roe buck found in someone's garden, that had probably been hit by a car, and whose hind leg had been so badly broken that the foot was twisted almost all the way round. The bone was protruding from the fetlock,

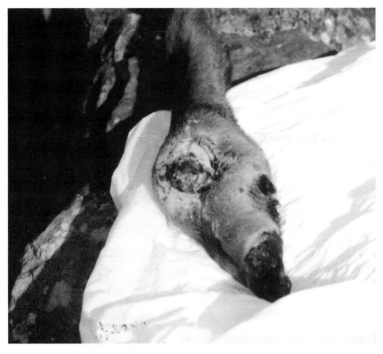

Broken leg

and the wound was gangrenous. There was obvious internal damage too, for the whole deer stank, and was obviously starving to death. He was not even fit for dog food, poor thing, and goodness knows how long he had been like that. Then there was another which had been belly-shot using an illegal weapon, which the dog found dying in the undergrowth on a farm I used to work regularly. Fortunately it had only just been hit, which meant I could end its suffering quickly, and the meat was not ruined. It was probably the most unpleasant gralloching (gutting) job I have ever had, as the expanding bullet had liquefied most of its insides. That incident illustrated just how far a mortally-hit deer can run, for it had certainly not been shot on the farm where it had been found. It is quite common to pick up deer with missing feet, or legs which have been broken and then healed, which is often the result of traffic accident and sometimes from being caught up in a fence. Sometimes a deer is still alive when you find it caught in a fence, and it needs to be shot then and there. I also used to use a brace of my dogs to run through silage just before it was cut, to send out the deer and save the fawns from being killed in the machinery, for otherwise they just lie still. If you drive out a silage field this way every day for a few days, the deer will usually move somewhere else of their own accord, and again, the best way to do this is with a dog, for the deer will seldom bother about farm vehicles or even a horse and rider, but a dog will find them every time.

Species

There are six species of deer found wild in the UK nowadays, plus one hybrid, but only two of these, the roe and the red, are native species. Distribution is irregular, though roe and fallow are found almost everywhere, and muntjac are colonising the land far more rapidly than perhaps we realise.

Muntjac
These interesting-looking small deer have been established in the wild in the UK for some time, and are steadily encroaching on

Muntjac

new ground. They are shy and elusive, preferring to stay in very thick cover, especially banks of brambles. If found in the open, they are easily picked up by a lurcher, but if cornered in cover, they can inflict a fair bit of injury with their small hooked antlers, and especially the long tusks which are bourne by both sexes There are two subspecies which can probably interbreed: the Reeves, which is the smaller, and the Indian, which has quite a reputation for attacking dogs, though both types can be pugnacious. They breed all year round, and therefore have no closed season. Seen out in the open, the 'Munty' causes a moment's puzzlement with its hunched, piglike appearance at odds with its red-brown coat, and especially when caught in the lamp at night, it can be a second or two before you realise what it is. Munty are the most delicious eating, and supply a good, fleshy carcase.

Chinese Water Deer

Another introduced species, these deer are at time of writing mostly found in the Bedfordshire/East Anglia area, though they are begin-ning to spread further afield and sightings have been reported in the Thames valley. Rare in their own natural habitat, English Nature estimates that twenty-five per cent of the world population of Chinese Water Deer is in England. They are extraordinarily prolific breeders, normally having two or three fawns at a time, though 'litters' of six have been recorded. Fenland farming suits them very well, so there are no restrictions on their control if they are causing damage or need thinning out locally. Chinese water deer lie up in scrub, marshland and rushes, similar to their natural habitat in China and Korea, rather than woodland, so a dog is ideal for finding them. Neither sex has antlers but instead both have long canine tusks. Unlike the Munty, the Chinese water deer can move these tusks a little, flicking them back out of the way when eating, and forward ready for action when threatened. Chinese water deer are also fast and agile, and not as simple to catch as they might at first seem. Some rate them as challenging as a hare to pursue and catch with a running dog. A lesser-known defensive attribute is the easily-shed coat, leaving a dog choking on a thick mouthful of loose hair if it gets its strike wrong.

Roe

Roe live in groups rather than herds, and are often found in twos and threes, enjoying the bed-and-breakfast facilities of woodland adjacent to farmland. These are probably the most popular and definitely the easiest deer for a single lurcher to take – and in fact almost any breed of dog that is of working type i.e. has not had its

JD 2005

Leaping roebuck

body so distorted by breeding for fashion that it is unable to function normally, can catch roe. These attractive deer are supposed to
be the fastest British mammal, but in my experience they are not
particularly fast in the open – though they can blast through cover
faster and more safely than any dog – and also aren't very clever
under pursuit. They have a tendency to run into danger rather than
out of it, run in circles, and even trip up and fall for no discernable
reason. While experienced deerstalkers have a raft of gizmos to help
them get close enough to roe for a safe shot, are out of bed before
dawn and have to use every ounce of their fieldcraft, dog owners
who are trying to avoid meeting deer have no end of trouble in roe
country. I have been hare-coursing under NCC rules, and seen the
same trio of roe forsake the quiet and safety of the woods to go
through the beat every hour or so, past a line of beaters and two
rows of screaming Greyhounds, a crowd of spectators and a packed
car park. I have been walking along a busy footpath at lunchtime
on a Bank Holiday Sunday and had a roebuck erupt out of cover,
leap a stock fence (behind which it had been safe) and land in the
middle of five dogs.

A friend was exercising his Greyhounds in the middle of a large

Head of roebuck

field when a roebuck ran right up to him, and once I was standing on a path with my dog on a lead when a roe ran up to us, slipped and went hooves up right at my feet, while I dragged a very indignant dog away, who could have caught it with slack in her lead and commented very loudly about this. Roe will run a short distance and then bark defiance, which tells the dog exactly where they are, and anyone else listening as well. In the days when I did deer work, I had a lot of permission on roe, and they really did not provide much of a challenge to the dog. Indeed, only a short while ago, I met a twenty-inch high Whippet lurcher with a badly broken front leg that had healed crookedly, who still coursed and caught roe with no trouble. Roe deer are very good eating and a reasonable size for one person to transport across country to a vehicle. To my way of thinking, they are the perfect quarry for a single lurcher, and my dogs seemed to agree with me as well, for they never needed formal entering and were adept at finding roe wherever they were lying up. I would see the dog's head go up, she would sniff the wind and look at me in a certain way, and I had about one second before it was lead on or game on.

One dog in particular was the most amazing finder and catcher of venison, even when slowed by age and injury. I remember in her eleventh year when she winded a trio of roe at the top of a punishing hill on one of the farms we used to hunt. 'She'll never get those' I thought, as she left my side, pelted all the way up the hill while the deer stood and watched her, circled them, picked the weak one and brought it through a hedge and all the way down the hill, then through a crop of standing oats where she lost quite a bit of ground and the deer bolted a fox. She stuck to her deer, launched it over the

Game on! (*E. Dearden*)

129

ditch and it came flat out towards me – if I had been a dog, it would have been perfectly placed for a kill, but as I am merely a human, I was unable to stop it. My poor bitch was furious: all that work, and I had failed her! She certainly could sulk, that dog: I was in disfavour for the whole day over that, and she could barely move for the next two. JB was mainly Deerhound bred, with a touch of Saluki, not the easiest dog to handle, but a consummate hunter, and she lived for catching deer. She once cleared five farms of roe for me, and we ate like kings.

Fallow

Fallow seen in the wild today are thought to be the result of deer-park escapees, and there are plenty of them. They come in a variety of colours from pure white, cream, shades of brown and red spotted with white, to black. They are a compact, meaty deer, and as good eating as roe, while distinctly differently flavoured. While a medium-sized dog can drop a fallow, it takes a strong dog to hold one, so what is needed is one with the knack of killing with its first strike. Fallow live in herds, and it is an education to see a dog set the herd moving and wait for the weakest deer to break away from the main group, just as the wolf pack will do with bigger deer, keeping just enough pressure on while keeping out of trouble. Fallow do not circle the way roe do, so the dog has to make its decision and take

Black Fallow

its deer quickly. Dogs that follow deer as opposed to coursing them with intent to catch can be taken a long way after a Fallow, which in our overcrowded country means across roads and into all sorts of dangers. Fallow are not particularly fast: I used to have a horse that loved to chase them, admittedly an ex-racehorse, but he could easily overtake them even with a rider on his back. There wasn't a thing I could do to stop him, and he clearly thought the whole affair was good fun, for once alongside, he would try to ride the deer off like a polo pony. From my point of view, it was far too close to those sweeping antlers.

Fallow are heavy deer for one person to move, which is, in my opinion, all the more reason for using a dog that can bring them to book in a short sprint.

Sika
These are all the descendents of park escapees, and there are several subspecies, all of which interbreed. The Sika can also interbreed with our native Red deer. While not as spectacular as the Red deer, especially in the matter of antlers, the Sika is generally thought to be better eating, and certainly carries plenty of flesh. A larger dog is better for Sika, which tend to run straight and know where they are going. They need to be taken on the run, as once they turn at bay they can be formidable opponents, and they have an aggressive whistling roar rather like a stallion's scream that carries a long way and may cause interest in the sort of people you would rather not meet at that precise time.

Red Deer
The Monarch of the Glen, is our picture of the biggest mammal in the UK, though they are considerably bigger (and better eating) in the West Country than in Scotland because of superior forage as well as the improving nature of managing the herds by using the staghound packs. It is estimated that there are as many Red deer in the West Country in England as in the whole of the rest of the UK. It takes an exceptional single dog to tackle a Red deer and bring it to book humanely, and the height, reach and jaw needs to be close to that of the purebred Deerhound, though these are now being bred so tall for the show ring that there is a clear difference between working and show type developing. I doubt very much whether any dog could take a Red stag solo, and even using two or three would involve a lot of risk and perhaps not be as humane as desirable, though in the old days Deerhounds would be used in pairs on the stags, and there are many old tales of exciting courses. Hinds are a more sensible quarry, and as with all females, far better eating,

Red deer stag

stag venison often being strong-smelling and rather stringy. Very few running dogs are used on Red deer nowadays, the logistics of moving the carcase being every bit as challenging to the human as the deer is to the dog.

Defence

Having evolved as a prey species, deer have a number of useful defence tactics, and the deer dog needs to be equal to these. Primary defence is running away, and the random leaps that a deer makes when running in the open are intended to throw the dog off its stride so that it cannot get itself in the right position to strike. Deer found out in the open will run to places where the dog will have difficulty in following. Woodland is a prime example, and deer will flicker in and out of close-set trees seemingly without losing speed, where the fast dog is in great danger of hitting a tree or being impaled on a broken branch. To see a fat roe go sideways through a barbed-wire fence, unscathed, is really something, and unless your dog has been wise to these fences from puppyhood, you could have a trip to the vet rather than venison on your mind when this happens. Deer will outrun a dog downhill, especially on rough and steep ground, and on flinty surfaces their hooves take little damage where the dog will slice her pads and, if you are unlucky, a tendon too. Being taller than the dog, the deer will crash through standing crops, game cover or tall heather, leaving the dog floundering. Small deer such as Muntjac will head for the thickest thorn and bramble cover that they can find, and face the dog down from inside it, where the dog is at a disadvantage. Red deer especially will head for water, known as 'soiling', where the dog or hound has to swim but the deer has the advantage of its superior height. Fallow are known for dropping down in cover, from where their scent is so little once they lie still that even an experienced pack of Buckhounds can draw right over them. You know he went in, you know he didn't come out, but he can't be found – and foolish is the human who tries, for a big buck erupting out of the bracken can make you feel very small indeed. It is amazing how flat a deer that is intent on concealment can go, and I've seen them flushed from cover that you wouldn't have thought would hide a rabbit, as well as suddenly barging out of a small hedge amid a starburst of blackbirds.

At Bay

Unless you are shooting, you do not want your deer to stand at bay. This is not the action of a deer which is exhausted, but that of a strong deer that is ready to kill the dog. Primary defence now is the long-reaching front feet, which can easily crush the skull of or cripple a dog; luckily dogs mostly realise this and keep well back. A running deer is easy for a dog to take, but at bay the dog is in

Lurcher pup practising with cast antler

danger: both dog and deer know it. Antlers are not a primary defence, for if they were, both sexes would sport them, and all year round as well; the main use of antlers is in fighting other male deer. Nevertheless, if the deer is antlered, you would do well to show these appendages respect: they certainly know how to use them, and they can do a deal of damage. Where roebuck antlers are stabbing spikes, Fallow antlers are big, wide and palmated, and it is tricky to avoid being caught by them if you have a big buck down. Sika antlers, while inferior to Red deer antlers in the matter of weight and general appearance, have long thin points which can cause appalling damage, and the magnificent weaponry of a Red deer stag needs no introduction. Any deer that has learned to kill a dog with its antlers will be committed to doing the same again, which is why it is so important to have a dog that can take the deer properly. Never, whatever the deer, try to restrain one by getting hold of an antler: the deer is far stronger than you, and the least you'll get away with is the skin taken off your hands.

From time to time, there is a freak accident between dog and deer, and one such happened in my area a few years ago. A pet lurcher that was in the habit of chasing deer disappeared after a roe buck and was found several days later, dead and dangling from one antler by his collar. This had so incapacitated the buck that he was almost dead when he was found on a nearby farm. The farmer shot the buck, and contacted the dog's owner so that she knew what had happened to her dog, which was very decent of him.

Tackling the Deer

So long as the deer is running, the dog has an excellent chance of bringing it down. This is not, as some would have you believe, an issue of strength, but rather that of knack, using the deer's own speed and strength to grass it just as a small person trained in one of the martial arts can bring a big person to the ground using little strength and much technique. People who haven't seen the deer job done properly think they should equip themselves with powerful, large-headed dogs, believing that they look the part, but that is not what you need in a deer dog at all. It is all a matter of balance and timing. A fast dog is far better for this job, as she can run well within herself until the time is right to take her deer, and a long lean jaw has a better reach than a thick broad one.

Different dogs use different methods, purely from instinct, and there is often a 'breed preference' depending on what the dog's ancestry is. Some dogs run alongside the deer's shoulder, wait until both its forelegs are off the ground and then shoulder-charge it, gripping the throat as the deer comes down. The deer's own weight plus the speed and force of the fall will break its neck in most cases, and the whole of the throat is torn out as well. Deerhound crosses are especially adept at this, and a tall dog will leap for the throat and bump the shoulder at the same time, quicker than the eye can register. The deer is dead quickly, and the meat is not damaged. Other dogs will trip the deer from behind, either gripping briefly just above the hock, or knocking one hind foot across behind the other. Done correctly either method is a matter of technique not strength. It is extremely effective provided the dog has the ability to follow through by leaping the falling body and taking out the throat, again breaking the neck in most cases. Only once did my JB fail to kill on impact, when a roe deer hesitated before jumping a fence and she did not have the room to manoeuvre it as she would have liked. Having downed it, she took it by the chin and pulled its head backwards, taking the whole deer in a circle belly-out. This meant that it could not touch her with antlers or hooves, and I was able to

An accomplished roe dog

administer the *coup de grâce* safely and easily. Pure instinct on the part of the dog, and very effective. Some years after this, I was reading *Jock of the Bushveldt* by Sir Percy Fitzpatrick, and noted that his crossbred Bull terrier used exactly the same technique when holding a wounded antelope that his master had shot. A deer on the ground will kick like fury, and I knew a dog with a scar from the hoof where each cleat had gone either side of his eye, and one of his teeth had been broken in another encounter.

I have seen a purebred Saluki take her deer by leaping on top of it while it was galloping, gripping the neck and dropping off, which somersaulted the deer, breaking its neck instantly. All of these methods are quick and humane, don't ruin the meat and cause the minimum of distress to the deer. Until a deer has been caught, being chased is not a matter of fear to it, because it has always previously been able to run away, but the interval between capture and death must be kept as short as possible if we are to respect ourselves as hunters. Some dogs hold rather than kill, which can lead to difficulties unless the owner is close at hand, for if a dog elects to hold the hock rather than the throat, or the nose in the way JB did, the deer will be distressed and the dog may be injured. There may also be a great deal of noise. I knew a big Deerhound type who would drop his deer and then lie on it, which, as he was only used on Roe, was pretty effective, though in the early stages of his career he had so much faith in me that he tended to get up as soon as I laid a hand on the quarry! Like most Deerhound crosses, and indeed, pure Deerhounds, he had no further interest in the quarry once it was down; luckily we never lost one and he soon learned to stay holding the deer down until I had despatched it. If your dog is the type to hold rather than kill, you must in all decency possess the equipment, the will and the skill to finish the job quickly and humanely. If your dog is one of those few that does not effect a good kill but bites at the deer when it is down, inflicting suffering and damage, then do not work that dog on deer again. It is unforgivable to cause such distress to your quarry, whatever you hunt, and if the dog does not have the skill and the courage to take deer cleanly, then it is not right to use her on them.

Possibly the best description that I have ever read on the taking of deer is in Kenneth Cassel's book about the Scottish Deerhound

Scottish Deerhound
(*C. Welch*)

A Most Perfect Creature of Heaven and refers to his sapling, Kirsty, on her first Red deer, having been started on blue hare and then taken a few roe. I quote the following passage by kind permission of the author, and also the British Deer Society, in whose journal it first appeared.

> Kirsty was pure show bred. None of her ancestors had worked for perhaps a hundred years. She stood 30 and a half inches at the shoulders and weighed 85 lb in running trim . . . A stalker on the West coast deer forest (Murdo) had shown interest in my dog and had enquired about her working ability. I therefore took Kirsty over and from behind his cottage we spied the hill. Various parties of deer were seen but by good luck one hind was lying in a position which, from the angle from which we would have to approach, would have the effect of making her the only beast in sight – an important consideration when using a sighthound. The stalk was not a difficult one; dead ground for the first half mile, then an increasingly prostrate crawl up a burn and then up its tributary. Cautiously we wriggled out over the bank. Seventy yards away and below us an ear flicked above the tall heather. I felt Kirsty stiffen beside me and begin to shiver. Ten yards were covered and then the hind was on her feet – one startled glance and away. I was not conscious of slipping Kirsty but there she was streaking across the heather in that deceptively leisurely Deerhound gallop in which each stride is some eighteen feet or so. Murdo had brought Kirsty and me in from above as he would for a rifle, which was a tactical error for a hound; hounds being lighter than the deer are better slipped uphill. Placed as we were, the hind had no choice but to go down and down she went over a very rocky and precipitous slope at a speed I would not have thought possible. She had a sixty yard start at the top but by the time she came out to the undulating floor of the glen she had increased this to some three hundred yards.
>
> Murdo was clearly disappointed and more or less prepared to write Deerhounds off there and then. Fortunately the glen was long and wide and quite open so that from half way up one side we had a clear view. Once Kirsty was out of the rocks she really set down to gallop. She began to pull up on her quarry as if there were an elastic band stretched between them. It was at this stage that Murdo's English deserted him and he began exclaiming in Gaelic in his excitement. Rapidly the distance closed. Through my glasses I saw Kirsty range up alongside, gallop for perhaps twenty yards level with the hind's shoulder and then suddenly make her leap. There was a wild flurry of movement as the two animals cartwheeled through the air and it was all over. Kirsty sniffed her dead quarry for a minute or

two, but did not touch it again and then trotted back to where the course had started. On examination there was no mark on the hind at all except the one terrific bite behind the head and the utterly broken neck. 'The jaws she must have!' said Murdo.

Meat

Venison is too delicious to miss, and most people hunting deer for pest control use the carcase in their own larder if the landowner (to whom it belongs by law) does not want it. Although there was once a ready market for venison, it is more difficult to sell to butchers and game dealers now because of all the paperwork required, and 'back-door' selling to pubs and restaurants is not always practical or indeed legal. Dressing out a deer carcase is not complicated – just hang it up and treat it as a large rabbit. There are complicated legalities attached to the taking of deer and the time of year, even the time of day, which it is useful to keep abreast of, and these apply even if you are culling the deer for pest control purposes. In culinary terms, as has been stated earlier, the female of the species is always much better eating, young venison is better than old, and only an idiot would tackle a rutting buck, for though they are fat at the start of the rut, they rapidly dwindle down to a tough, stringy and rank-smelling carcase which is not worth the effort. Buck in the rut are very much more aggressive, and usually another buck is not far away. Being bold and careless, should a rutting buck need to be culled, it usually presents a relatively straightforward shot, and that is the best fate for it.

Caveat

Before you ever start your lurcher on deer, think well, for the disadvantages may well outweigh the advantages, and I speak as one who has done a lot of deer work. The deer is such a supremely natural quarry that there is no going back once your dog has started on them, and most lurchers will wed to this quarry with such a passion that they will take deer in preference to anything else. You cannot tell the dog that what is welcome on this farm is not on that; the dog has no concept of boundaries or human laws, nor any understanding that today you are after a different quarry. She will leave the netted rabbit buries to sail over a fence and pursue a deer, she will wind deer and find them when out on exercise, she will come off the quarry you have chosen for her on the lamp and speed off into the darkness on the heels of a deer, she will spin them over wherever she encounters them. If you are happy with this, fine, but if it is likely to give you problems in the future, think well, because once this particular box has been opened, you will never get the lid on it again.

Unlike fox and hare (and, surprisingly, sometimes rabbit) the committed deer dog will not tire of her quarry, quit because it is too much effort, or become afraid of it. If she escapes injury from running through woodland or over the dangerous terrain that a deer will take her through, and she knows her job, she will be taking deer into her dotage, which means an ever-increasing risk of injury from the deer when her body is no longer capable of making that vital leap. Owning a deer dog means for ever being on the alert for deer, even if you are just out for a short walk, and believe me, you can find them in some unusual places. I have encountered red deer in suburban back gardens, on housing estates, and even the central reservation of a busy dual carriageway. I have been in the annoying position of working land where I had full permission to take deer, and being so placed to take one easily, but being unable to because of the close proximity of other people who would have caused more fuss and bother than the catch would be worth. On some occasions, these people were even trespassing, as was the case with a straying dog-walker who commented indignantly that 'your dog nearly had that deer!' I remember flushing a deer out of a wood just right, and it ran so close to my colleague that he could have touched it as it passed, but a neighbour was trimming his hedge right on the boundary, and we had to leave it go. It is a given fact that if your dog is coursing a deer in a place where it should not, the field will be the brightest emerald green, the deer will be the shiniest russet and the dog will sparkle like a diamond in the cheery rays of the sun.

You can steady a dog to deer that has never had one, but once the dog has taken this quarry, there is no going back. A single dog can be of great value if she takes her deer well: she can protect crops and provide meat over a wide area and several years. If you own one, you may find her services on request almost more than you can fulfil, in the right area. Or you may suffer the most exquisite varieties of embarrassment, even brushes with the law, depending on where you are.

6 Miscellaneous Fur and Feather

Small Vermin and Gamebirds

Being such versatile dogs, lurchers can be an asset in the control of small vermin as well as their more high-profile quarry. Good inroads into populations of rats, mink, stoats and grey squirrels can be made with the assistance of a lurcher of any size and breeding. The only caveat is that if you hunt mainly for the table, using your lurcher on small, biting quarry can make the dog hard-mouthed. If you hunt purely for pest control, then this is not an issue. Entering to this type of quarry is better done with another dog

A solid grounding in rabbit work

which knows the score, for many lurchers will get bitten the first time, unless they are instinctively programmed to bite and shake. Terrier and Whippet crosses seem to have this inborn, whereas collie types may sustain a nip or two before they get their blood up. For this reason, it is better to have a solid grounding in rabbit work before progressing to small vermin.

Mice

I found by far the best way to start is with mice. Although mice will bite, it is nothing in comparison to a bite from larger rodents, not to mention mustelids. Out in the fields, especially in autumn, mice will be on or just under the surface, and your dog will quite naturally hunt them, springing into the air like a mousing vixen, following with a quick snap. You may get the result retrieved to hand, or the dog might swallow the mouse. Apart from being sure to keep up with your dog's worming programme in the latter case, it really doesn't matter which happens, though do be aware if you take a live one from your dog that a mouse can climb up its own tail at great speed and deliver a memorable bite! My pups usually start themselves off on mice without any input from me, and indeed I have had a six-week-old lurcher pup kill and retrieve mice, though I could have done without the one delivered to me on my pillow. If, like me, you lead a rural sort of life, you will be accustomed to the autumnal mouse incursions every year once the crops have been cut and again when the weather starts to turn cold. We have had many sporting runs in the confines of the kitchen, sometimes with the addition of a ferret to get the little devils out from behind the washing machine. It doesn't matter how much large quarry work your lurcher does, she will still remain keen on mice, and even old retired dogs will find and catch these, and be very pleased with themselves that they can still be useful.

Mice will also be dug out from their homes in the fields, and you can only marvel at the nose of a dog, that they can smell a mouse underground (or maybe the mice stink?). Lurcher paws are very good at digging – you may have noticed this from excavations in your garden – and they can shift a fair amount of spoil in a short time. Often, the mouse flies out with the earth, to sneak away while the lurcher is snorting threats down the hole. This can make for hilarious hunting if you view the mouse away and try to get the lurcher out of the crater in time to see it. Several dogs together will get in each other's way and have a grand time mousing; it is good training for them to obey you as well, because a dog that is slow to respond will lose its mouse.

Quite the best mouse hunting I have ever had was in a derelict farmyard that was absolutely overrun with them. We would go into an outbuilding, shut the door if possible, and having made sure that our trouser bottoms were tucked firmly into our socks, start lifting the mounds of old sacks and other debris with sticks. Dogs soon learned to watch what was happening, and to snap up the mice as they burst out of cover. The mice would ping through the air – mice are amazingly athletic – run up walls and scurry along the floor while the dogs spun and leaped to catch them. Small dogs have the advantage in a confined space, but large lurchers can be mouse-hounds too, and we caught incredible numbers of mice. Such were the quantities that the dogs soon gave up swallowing their catch, just crunching and spitting them out to get the next one. As well as doing a useful, humane job, it was a breathless process, and we would end up convulsed with laughter as we tried to dodge bat-talions of mice. It didn't take us long to get numbers right down, then the agent who was selling the property thanked us and warned that he would be putting poison down for the remainder of the mice. That was the end of our side of the operation, which was a pity from our point of view but of course we had been lucky to have had the 'mousing rights' at all. Though I have caught mice on other farms and warehouses since, nothing was quite the experience of those mouse-infested outbuildings.

Rats

Rats are readily come across wherever you walk with your dog, and in addition can be found in large concentrations on many types of farm and industrial units. Waterways almost always have a rat population. Ratting can be opportunistic, or you may be a member of a ratting group or club where hunting arrangements are more formal. Rats can be flushed from their holes using smoke, or ferrets, or else a ratting team can drive a rat-infested area as if it was a game crop. Terriers are the traditional ratting dogs, but lurchers can become very adept, and Whippets are excellent ratters too, with the agility and commitment to equal any other dog. I have had enor-mous fun lamping rats at night using a lurcher and an air rifle though I only ever have one or two people along if someone is shooting, and only one person using the gun. Rats are bolder at night and easier to find, especially once you have found their regular runs along beams and so on. Anyone that you have along on a ratting trip must be sensible and reliable. Although sticks are handy for lifting up debris under which rats might be hiding, or else persuading them to leap off high places, I personally discourage people from using sticks to hit rats. It is far too easy for a dog to be accidentally injured if people use sticks this way, and the dog is far more adept at catching rats than people are at hitting them. Rats are also remarkably hard to kill cleanly this way. Sticks can be handy for rattling rats out of drain-pipes and enclosed machinery, often into the waiting jaws of a handy dog.

Rat Training

Rats being intelligent beasts, they can be trained quite easily. One person I know had the brainwave of putting food out for the rats and then playing a particular piece of music very loudly. It was only a matter of days before the rats would come out and search eagerly for food as soon as they heard the music start. Once the rats were satisfactorily trained, they were dealt with. You can obviously only do this once with any rat colony, so make the most of it.

Team Players

The late Dr Brian Plummer had a passion for ratting, at which his eponymous terriers excelled, and he observed that if a pack of dogs went ratting as a team on a regular basis, they would split duties into 'find' dogs and 'catch' dogs. If one of the key 'finders' or 'catchers' was not in the pack for some reason, then another dog would change roles, so it was quite possible for a dog to perform either task. This is what you want with your lurcher, so if she is showing a tendency to become one or the other, swap around from time to time so that she has a chance to develop both aspects of her hunting ability.

Starting

Lurchers taken ratting must have their adult teeth through and set, and although pups of eight or nine months old can make excellent ratters, personally I believe in waiting a little longer unless the dog has a lot of terrier in her. Of course, sometimes opportunity presents itself inconveniently early. One of my Deerhound-bred pups faced her first rat when she was only a few weeks old: she still had her milk-teeth, and not much jaw power. As a consequence, she sustained a nasty bite that went right into her tiny nose. By the time I had heard her squawk and come rushing round the corner to see what was the matter, she had killed the rat. The experience might easily have put her off, but luckily she was a feisty sort, and though she killed many rats as well as far larger animals, she never was bitten by small vermin again.

Looking for rats

Health

Rats carry some unpleasant diseases which they will happily share with us as well as our dogs, the chief of which is Leptospirosis or Weil's Disease, sometimes known as 'rat-catcher's yellows' for the jaundice that sufferers develop. Spread by rat urine, Weil's can kill, and will certainly make you feel very ill indeed even if it doesn't. Therefore you must take certain precautions if you frequent ratty places. There is no human vaccination for Weil's, and the canine sort lasts for three to six months and only covers two of the many varieties found. Research done in America indicates that the bulk of adverse reaction seen in vaccinated canines comes from the leptospirosis vaccine, all of which leaves dog owners in a rather difficult position when deciding whether or not to have their dogs vaccinated. I am certainly not going to attempt to advise you what to do; I can only suggest that you research the whole issue very thoroughly – your vet may not have the time to keep up with current findings – and base your decision on all the information you can get. Perhaps by the time your dog is ready to start ratting, there will be better treatment available than at present. Meanwhile, change your clothes and footwear as soon as you get back from a ratting expedition, wash the one in very hot water and disinfect the other, and don't eat your sandwiches with ratty hands. I have spent much of my life working in rat-infested areas, as have my dogs; either we have been very lucky or we have built up some sort of immunity. This disease must be taken very seriously, so in addition to whatever other precautions you take, only go ratting when you and your dog are healthy and don't overload your immune systems. If you or any of your dogs develop suspicious symptoms after a ratting trip, be sure to get treatment straight away. Puppies are especially vulnerable to Weil's, so if you have a litter of puppies at home, don't run the risk of bringing the disease back to them, and do everything possible to ensure that your own home and garden is rat-free before the bitch whelps.

Grey Squirrels

The tree rat, the grey squirrel, causes serious problems both to forestry and bird populations, killing trees by barking them, and taking eggs, fledglings and even adult birds when the opportunity presents itself. They will also cause a great deal of damage should they get into your loft and start chewing on the wiring. They are

Mixed – and very successful – squirreling team

mainly responsible for the massive decline in the red squirrel population in the UK, not only because they carry 'squirrel pox' which affects reds more than greys, but because they are able to survive on a more varied diet. They eat the food that the reds rely on – such as hazelnuts, which grey squirrels eat in the unripe condition, but reds prefer ripened – and then the reds have had their food supply decimated while the greys go on to eat something else. As an introduced species, they must not, by law, be released once they have been caught, and it is important for ecological reasons to kill as many grey squirrels as possible. They are one of the few species for which it is legal at the time of writing to use poison. In their native North America, grey squirrels are considered good eating, though for some reason this has not really caught on in the UK. I can vouch for their being delicious, surprisingly fleshy for their size, with white meat that lends itself well to creamy, mushroomy sauces. Served raw and in the jacket, ferrets really like them, too. However, squirrels are the devil to skin, best done while still warm if you can, or else put in the freezer after you have paunched them, when the skin comes off more easily after thawing. Because it is legal to poison squirrels, never eat or give to your ferrets any that you have not shot or caught yourself, or otherwise know to be healthy. A squirrel dozy enough to have been hit by a car probably had something wrong with it beforehand.

Squirrels are most often caught by lurchers on an opportunistic basis while walking in the woods. Young squirrels especially can be caught out while they are fossicking about on the ground, and a quick, agile dog, maybe with a lot of Whippet in it, is ideal for scooping these up. I have a Bedlington lurcher who is something of a squirrel expert, and once bounded partway up the side of a knapped-flint church wall to catch his squirrel, before falling off. Yes, I had trouble believing it too.

If you are part of a drey-poling or drey-poking team, the addition of a lurcher can be very useful. Not only will they pick up and despatch any injured squirrels, but their very presence will attract the squirrel's attention so that it will concentrate on keeping the tree-trunk between itself and the dog, which can often result in a good shooting opportunity for the human side of the arrangement. A dog will see the squirrels more easily than the humans, and get them moving along the tree canopy where, silhouetted against the sky, they will offer a better shot. Squirrels have long teeth and pack an evil bite, and dogs pretty soon learn to despatch them before they can try it. I once had a squirrel retrieved alive and unharmed to hand, and I can tell you that it concentrates the mind wonderfully being presented with that. Squirrels also house some of the

147

'One up here'

hungriest fleas, even worse than cat fleas in terms of their liking for human blood, and I have learned to let carcases cool and fleas depart before I take them home.

'It's down here now'

Mink hunting sequence

Mink

This is another North American import which has found itself a destructive niche in UK ecology. Again, by law, a mink must not be released once caught. These vicious little predators wreak havoc on land, in water and up trees, and have even caused local extinction of vulnerable species such as water voles, upon which a lot of other creatures, such as owls, depend. It is therefore incumbent upon those of us who are able to do so to kill as many mink as we can.

Mink are most usually found along waterways, and I have had some terrific hunts on mink with a mixed pack of lurchers and terriers, as well as the memory of great days out with different packs of minkhounds. Mink will readily take to trees if the pursuit becomes too hot, or else dive when cornered in water, and it is a good dog that can take mink regularly. I live near flood plains, and mink are sometimes found in fields near flooded ares, which can make for some lively hunts. If you are in a position to handle a live mink, don't: they have a bite out of all proportion to their size, and can turn around in their skins to deliver it, going through the stoutest gloves as if they were butter.

Stoats and Weasels

These smaller cousins of the mink don't do anything like as much damage, and can be tolerated in some areas where there are no vulnerable species, but where there are gamebirds, free-range poultry or rare wild species, stoats and to a lesser extent weasels, have to be culled. Normally solitary, you can come across family groups in the summer, and they are fascinating to watch. Most rabbiters have seen a stoat pursuing a rabbit in the manner of a miniature hound, nose to the ground, purposefully and relentlessly trotting after the poor beast, which is often frozen with terror by the time the stoat strikes. Some rabbits are made of sterner stuff, though, and I have also seen stoats bucked off and kicked to death by a determined rabbit.

So far as your lurcher is concerned, hunting these small mustelids is again a matter of opportunity. They must carry a strong scent, for I have seen dogs 'drag' up to them over quite a distance. They certainly have a strong scent once caught, for like mink and other mustelids, they fire their scent glands under duress, and the resulting pong will linger on your dog for a couple of days. Dogs will dig stoats and weasels out of shallow underground tunnels and make short work of them. Being a small, fast-moving target, these are not always so easy to shoot, and a lurcher is as useful as a terrier for bringing them to book if wounded.

If you work your lurcher to ferrets, it makes sense to have her absolutely steady to them before you branch out into mink and stoats. Though they look similar if you see them in a hurry, they all smell different, even to a human nose, and a dog will have no trouble making the distinction between that which she should catch, and that which needs to be left alone, just as long as you are sure to teach her the difference rather than just leaving it to chance.

Moles

By no stretch of the imagination can the mole be considered a lurcher's regular quarry, or that of any other dog, but some individuals become accomplished molers. They can hear a tunnelling mole when it is approaching the surface, and will dig furiously, then seize the mole and despatch it. It has to be said that they probably do more damage in the garden than the mole, but even so, it is an admirable trait.

Mole

Feather

Part of a lurcher's remit was always to take feathered quarry. Either they take to it straight away or they have to be coaxed into it with some skill, using the tricks of a good gundog trainer – wings sewn onto a dummy, frozen game, fresh game contained in a stocking, then with holes made in the stocking and the wings brought through. Eventually, the reluctant retriever of feather will become competent to the job, and if desired, may be further trained to take feathered game from water. A few will not pick feather at all, and so you will have to forget that job for them. Some, however, are born to take feather, enter very early, and become artists at the job.

If you want your dog to take some kinds of feather but leave others – for instance, if you work your dog on keepered land, especially in the beating line – you will be pleasantly surprised at how quickly a lurcher will pick up on what must be ignored, what should be flushed and left, and what is fair game for catching. To see a lurcher leap maybe four feet in the air to snatch a rising pheasant is a spectacular experience, and I know one small Whippet/collie cross who is an expert at environmentally friendly duck, catching

Environmentally friendly mallard

them by the neck as they flush. Feathered game caught by a lurcher is much pleasanter to eat, as you are not risking your teeth on lead shot, or even worse, steel, bismuth or tungsten. A few lurchers become proficient in water as well as on land, not just gundog crosses, which is what you might expect, but collie and kelpie-bred dogs too. Those with a lot of sighthound are often less keen, but I have seen a purebred coursing Greyhound take to the water without hesitation. Generally speaking, the tall narrow-bodied dogs find water work physically more difficult than the rounder leg-at-each-corner shapes, though there will always be exceptions.

Gun Work

If your dog likes to retrieve to the gun, this is a good way to start her off on feather. Pigeons can be vexatious because the feathers are loose and come off easily in the mouth, so do the decent thing and help your lurcher to clean her lips after each retrieve. Most dogs take to pheasant and partridges straight away, and can point snipe as well as any gundog. They are useful finders of downed woodcock too, often liking them better than some gundogs. If you shoot winged vermin, you are likely to find your dog is less keen to carry

Working to the gun (*Roly Boughton*)

Retrieving a crow

these – they must taste awful. Mine will retrieve corvids, but you can see that they don't enjoy it, whereas gamebirds and wood-pigeons are brought back with glee. Lurchers are amazing as gundogs: my Bedlington cross is quite outstanding at finding shot game, even runners, though he has never been formally taught. Up goes the nose as soon as he hears the shot, off he goes when sent, and he is back just as fast. Should I then begin to glow with pride, I am rapidly brought back to earth by dint of his extremely hard mouth, which renders most retrieves, however stylish, as fit only for ferret food. This was especially noticable once when he was acciden-tally sent on a partridge while the Sahib was lamping him. 'Did he kill it?' I asked. 'Put it this way,' said my beloved, 'It was like the choke barrel at ten yards.'

Many years ago, when I was struggling badly financially, I acquired a little silver brindle bitch pup from the dog rescue, and she was some dog for catching pheasants. I lived on the edge of a big game shoot, and we would go picking-up at dusk on shoot days after everyone had gone home. She took any number of pricked pheasants for me, and probably uninjured ones as well, even catching them through stock-fencing, which handcuffed her to the fence until I could rescue her. I recall her once chasing a pricked pheasant as it flew about four feet off the ground over rough cover, giving her a very testing pursuit. The pheasant then took a glide over a lake, which the bitch did not see until too late, the result being pure drama. My poor dog disappeared in a great wave of water, then nothing broke the surface until a small dark arrow appeared, which was her head. She swam determinedly to the bank and then after a good shake and a sneeze or two, started hunting again. She lost that pheasant, but there were plenty more that day.

She caught me every sort of gamebird, and some unconventional ones, waterfowl too. With those and her rabbiting skills, she kept the pair of us fed through some very dark days. All of this was completely instinctive: I never had to teach her anything, and she was a dog who was supposedly 'unmanageable'. Times change, and I began to count gamekeepers as my friends, which meant not only were pheasants not for catching, but I would be given as many as I could use. Ever adaptable, the little bitch learned to flush them and leave them, and found new employment checking rearing and release pens for foxes and other vermin, while ignoring the pheasant poults and partridges. She was a lovely dog in every way, and the foundation bitch of the line I keep today.

Poultry

Steady the dog to domestic poultry early on, whether or not you keep it yourself, for you do not want problems in farmyards, and while tales of the traditional 'kannichor' (chicken thief) make good reading, there is no justification for stealing anyone's birds. The dog can tell hens from pheasants, and this will not harm her working potential. The only exception that I had was when I was working part-time at a poultry farm, which was excellent for henproofing my dogs, but unfortunately duckproofed them as well, for once steady to domestic duck, they would not look at mallard. Similarly, they saw no difference between domestic and wild geese. I remember one year when we had floods a pair of swans took up residence nearby, and would hiss and display at everybody who sploshed up the footpath. My Bedlington cross gave them a very superior look as he went past, not at all intimidated and clearly assuming them to be poultry. No doubt they'd have been very indignant, had they known.

7 Running Dogs of Australia and America

Kangaroos and Coyotes

The large running dogs still used in Australia and America came over in the first instance with the settlers, and the types of dog evolved, as in their homeland United Kingdom, with the kind of quarry, terrain and weather that they faced. Can these dogs be considered true lurchers? I will leave that to you to decide, but their work and the way they conduct it is far too important not to be acknowledged in this book.

Australia

Large sighthound types known as 'kangaroo dogs' evolved from baselines that were chiefly Deerhound and Greyhound, and no doubt with additional blood as it became available, bearing in mind the huge distances between settlements and the lack of transport in the early days. These dogs needed size to handle large quarry, speed to get up to it, and courage and dexterity to kill it without sustaining damage themselves. They had to be tough to handle extremes of weather, especially the heat, to perform on hard, rough ground, and to be worked often, being a chief provider of meat as well as protecting grazing for domestic stock. Less was needed in the way of intelligence and biddability, because the job was much more 'point and fire' and there was more space in which to do it. The modern 'roo dog needs the same attributes, plus considerable agility to handle the stock-fences that the quarry will leap, and the testing brush undergrowth that it will cross in an attempt to throw off its pursuer. Kangaroos being very fast, able to sustain speeds of around 40 mph, the modern hunter tends to use a pickup-type vehicle with good cross-country performance, carrying the dogs in the back, in boxes which have doors that can be opened from the cab. Leaping from a moving vehicle can be really hard on the dogs' legs and feet, and many owners prefer to halt the vehicle, having got into a favourable position, which puts more distance on the course but is better for the dogs in the long term.

Kangaroos, especially the males, can be aggressive, and put a dog in real danger. They can catch hold of a dog in their front feet, and then, sitting on their tails, disembowel it with a powerful kick from the hindlegs, which carry massive claws. Many kangaroo dogs are therefore run in wide collars which can give some protection if the claw catches in the collar instead of slashing down the dog's belly. Kangaroos will also sit back in water, catch the dog and drown it, much as a deer, the Old World equivalent, will stand at bay or 'soil' in water, and strive to strike down a dog with its front feet. To have a career on this quarry, dogs need to bring their 'roo down either by grabbing hold of its tail and then taking the throat once it is down, or by going straight at the neck as they range up alongside it. While many 'roo dogs can finish the job quickly on their own, they are often hunted in pairs or larger groups to speed up the catch and kill, and it is as well for the handlers to be close behind for those times when things do not go exactly to plan. The bush is a hard country for man and dog alike, the potential for injury is great, and dogs need to be tough in mind and body.

Kangaroos and wallabies are by no means the only quarry. Emus are hunted by 'roo dogs, which get the knack of taking them by the neck and killing them straight away. Emus can do a lot of damage

Steady to poultry

with a kick from one of their massively-clawed feet as well, so they are no sinecure. Foxes are a tremendous pest in Australia, and killed by every means, so dogs that can course and pick up a fox are very useful here as well. Although Australia has a great rabbit problem and some areas have hares, both imported by early settlers, there is not the tradition of using small lurchers on rabbit and hare that there is in the U.K., though in days gone by, there was a plethora of small coursing clubs which used Greyhounds on the brown hare to strict NCC rules. Small lurchers are generally not seen in Australia unless imported; rabbits are more usually controlled by other methods and any hare coursing done is unofficial, it having been banned some years ago.

Feral pigs are another pest in Australia, both to agriculture and ecology, and teams of crossbred dogs are used to hunt them in some areas. Strong dogs are needed, and pig dogs usually have such as Bull terrier, Pit bull, Rottweiller, Boxer or Mastiff in their ancestry. While a typical pig dog has more mass and strength than a 'roo dog, these latter can be useful as part of a pig-hunting team; Kenneth Cassels in *A Most Perfect Creature of Heaven* mentions purebred Deerhounds catching wild pig in Australia, but needing assistance in the despatching at times. Most pig-hunting dogs, however bred, hold the pig either physically or at bay ('bailing') and wait for their human team-mates to administer the *coup de grâce*, unless the pig is small. This is not strictly a job for the running dog, but few Australians carry passengers in their kennels, and whatever quarry gets up needs to be hunted.

America

The use of running dogs in America evolved similarly, with dogs being brought in by settlers and crossbred either in a deliberate attempt at bettering the type, or because that was all there was available to breed from in sparsely-populated areas. Famous names such as General Custer, Ernest Thompson Seton and Theodore Roosevelt were all eager aficionados of the running dog, and photographs show that these look very similar to strains of large lurcher found in Britain today. What was the 'roo dog in Australia became the staghound in America, not to be confused with the English staghound, which is a scent-hunting hound similar to a large Foxhound, and only worked in a pack to hunt the Red deer. The American staghound is chiefly a mixture of old Borzoi and Deerhound strains, mixed with 'cold-blood' (unregistered) Greyhounds, 'hot-blood' (track-bred) Greyhounds, sometimes

Saluki, and maybe a dash of scenting hound. The results are tested hard in the field, run chiefly on a variety of jackrabbits (hares), foxes and coyotes. Mostly they are worked in twos or threes (what the English would call 'a brace' or 'a leash' respectively) especially as far as the coyote is concerned, this animal being considered a serious test not just in the catching but in the despatching. As a recent arrival from Britain commented, 'A coyote is not a large fox – it is a small wolf.'

Mainly hunted in the mid and far West, the coyote weighs in at an average of thirty pounds, but larger specimens are not uncommon, forty pounders being found and even, rarely, up to fifty. Dutch Salmon, in his book *Gazehounds and Coursing* (High-Lonesome Books, Silver City, New Mexico) considers that the coyote does not twist and turn like the fox and is possibly not quite as fast, but has far greater stamina. If not caught within the first mile, it is unlikely to be caught at all, and has so much fight in it at the end that the pursuing hounds must have plenty left in reserve to finish it. Unlike with a fox, where the lift and shake is an integral part of the kill, the coyote's attacking powers need to be neutralised by the first dog getting hold of it by the neck and holding it down until one of the others can help despatch it by crunching through its chest. As with any running dogs, you get specialists, and there are coyote hounds bred from generations of coyote specialists that, while they can acquit themselves comfortably on other suitable quarry, really come into their own chasing the 'brush wolf'.

Foxes consist of (imported) red and (native) gray, the red behaving much as they do anywhere and needing good qualities in the dog of finding, coursing and despatching; the gray fox is not considered such a sporting quarry as it tends to run in short circles and go up trees when pursued, therefore favouring a different type of hound and maybe a gun as well. Where coyotes are present, they tend to sort out the fox population themselves, and very efficiently they do it, too. They are also not averse to entering human townships and taking dogs and cats that they find straying, or even when confined in their own backyard, which the coyote will enter apparently readily.

So far as rabbits and hares are concerned, there are several species. Jackrabbits are true hares, and Salmon mentions the blacktail or blueside jackrabbit, the whitetail jackrabbit, the antelope jackrabbit, the European brown hare and the varying hare (snowshoe rabbit). The true rabbits are referred to as 'cottontails' of which the Eastern cottontail and the desert cottontail are the most likely to be come across. These behave the same way as the UK rabbits in that they are sprinters into refuge rather than offering testing courses.

All the jackrabbits are excellent coursing quarry. Cottontails are not hunted with the fervour and delight that the British lurcher owner experiences, for there is no tradition of ferreting, long-netting or lamping, and American hunters are unlikely to go out specifically to catch rabbits the way we do in the UK. However, rabbits will pop up in front of dogs and give them a short sprint to cover, and a proportion will be caught in the usual sporting manner of the running dog.

Strangely enough, it is illegal in most American States to course deer.

Few dogs in Britain cover the kind of distances that these Australian and American dogs handle as frequently as they do, and can claim their level of toughness and fitness, especially in regard to the heat and hard going at some times, and the snow and bitter cold in others. As a result of this constant field testing, really admirable specimens have evolved and are a credit to the men and women who work them.

Epilogue

What is the appeal of lurcher work? It attracts people of all ages and backgrounds, some who come willingly and in full knowledge, others who are drawn spiritually to the beauty and symmetry of the lurcher, her sweet nature and easy company, without realising the instincts and abilities that lie just beneath the surface. I know many such who, all unknowing, acquired a lurcher and then a completely new way of life. Once anyone has experienced the world through a lurcher's presence and touched base with such pure and ancient values, they will never choose to leave it.

There are also those for whom lurchers are 'in the blood' through generations, with tales told at their elders' knees, and lurchers whose lines, deeds and names are a precious part of the family history. There are those who have only just dipped a toe in the water of lurcherdom, to whom the keeping of a dog is a new experience, never mind such a dog, so very different from more pedestrian breeds. Nobody knows everything about lurcher work, for each dog teaches us much that we never knew before, each run and every quarry similarly. All of us come to lurcher work with as much to learn, and every dog has as much to give. Lurcher owners are as diverse as the dogs they keep and the quarry they work. It is these wonderful, talented creatures that take us back to our true roots and those things that are important, who gift us with seeing the woods and fields, hills and valleys in a totally different way, and who take us to that place where past and future meld in a moonless night. Look into those huge, fathomless eyes, and know thyself.

Index